Accelerated Spanish

A Creative and Proven Approach, for Learn
Spanish Short Stories and Language Lessons

Anthony García

Table of Contents

Introduction

Are you one of those people who have been considering learning a new language? Is Spanish the one you are considering to learn?

In case you didn't know yet, Spanish is one of the most widely spoken languages in the world. More than five hundred million individuals are native Spanish speakers. Therefore, by that figure, it is considered as the second most sought-after language following Mandarin Chinese. Apart from that, a study has shown that it's the most romantic of all languages. No matter if you wish to learn the language simply to widen your knowledge or you simply want to learn it because you're traveling a Spanish-speaking destination, you will require a guide to make your whole learning process much simpler and stress-free.

This book is suitable for you, especially if you're not trying to pass a Spanish class. That's because it will get you speaking the language quick. In any scenario, you don't need to be a language professor just to speak the language. This book will surely teach you how to speak the language with the help of simple and practical examples. It will also walk you through discussions to help you get your point across whenever you are meeting new individuals, finding directions, going shopping, traveling, eating in a restaurant, and so much more. In short, this book will guide you on how to speak Spanish virtually in any sort of situation.

The good thing here is that you won't find boring grammar lessons and rules you wouldn't bother with anyway. As an alternative, you will explore many practical examples as well as notes, which will guide you on how to understand better how to speak. While the Spanish language isn't as complex to learn as English is, the language does have its quirks, you must be familiar.

You will find many reasons for desiring to learn the Spanish language. First, because being bilanguage will make you desirable in the job marketplace. It will also provide you a higher sense of self-confidence if you could step in and assist individuals who are having a difficult time with the language barrier out in public. Have you ever thought of how many instances you've seen somebody speaking the language and having trouble to communicate with other people? You wish you could help them but you can't. Today, you don't need just to stand there. You could finally step in and help both people.

Learning a new language like Spanish is advantageous to your self-value and resume as well. What's more, it is a wonderful way to keep your brain exercising. Some people don't stop learning. Therefore, learning a new language could be your initial step to continuing education.

As you now go on along with the learning journey, you'll discover different vital tips, which make will understanding and speaking the language much simple. Using this book, you could be talking Spanish in no time at all. Best of luck and buen viaje!

A. Method of Learning a New Language

Efficient language learners have a positive response when faced with the unfamiliar. Therefore, instead of letting yourself to feel pissed, confused, and frustrated every time listening to Spanish, why don't you try to keep a positive point of view? Start working to know anything you could. It could help you think of speaking in Spanish as a puzzle to be solved, or it could be an interesting challenge to be reached. Every time you hear spoken Spanish, you must concentrate on what is being told. Do not get distracted by your negative ideas. Listen for cognates that are words, which are similar or almost the same in two languages. Take note that English and Spanish share many cognates. Some of these are much / **mucho**; culture / **cultura**; aspect / **aspecto**; important / **importante**; professor / **professor**; introductory / **introductorio**; and course / **curso**.

B. The Spanish Language

The Spanish language is also called as **castellano** or **español.** This language was established in the Iberian Peninsula in the region of Castile. Spanish is considered as the third most spoken language in the world, according to the United Nations. Approximately, at least half a billion of folks speak the language. It is spoken on four continents and is the official language of twenty nations.

Aside from that, the language is also spoken more every year in the mainland of the U.S. In fact, approximately forty million individuals in the U.S. speak the language at home. That makes up over twelve percent of the population of the country. A 2015 report conducted by a government organization in Spain sowed that there are more Spanish speakers in the U.S. compared there to Spain.

You will find three major differences, which determine how this language is spoken in one region versus another. This includes grammar, accent, and vocabulary. The differences in vocabulary lead in various words utilized in various locations to refer to a similar thing. For instance, the word "the computer" in Latin America is **la computadora**. Meanwhile, you will say it in Spain as **el ordenador**.

When we talk about the accent, you will find some variances among regions. You will also find differences between regions in a similar country. The most evident difference in accent among those Spanish speaker connects to the way to say the letter **z**, the letter **c** then followed by **e** or **i**.

Another example is in Latin America, the letter **z, as well as the letter,** mixes **ci** and **ce** are spoken along with an **s** sound. On the other hand, in central and northern Spain, it was spoken along with **th** sound. For instance, the term for "shoe" is **zapato**. In Latin America, it is uttered as **sapato.** In Madrid, it is spoken as **thapato.**

You might not notice many grammatical differences among regions. However, there are some, which deal with the plural form of "you." In both Latin America and Spain, the term **ustedes** is the formal and plural way to talk "you." Meanwhile in Spain, you will find an informal and plural way to utter "you." **Vosotras** in the feminine while **vosotros** in the masculine. However, **vosotras** and **vosotros** aren't utilized in Latin America. As an alternative, **ustedes** is utilized for the plural "you" in every scenario.

Regardless of such differences in grammar, accent as well as vocabulary, thousands of Spanish speakers converse efficiently across every region where the language is pronounced. Even those speakers of Spanish from various countries understand one another totally well.

C. How to Pronounce the Vowels

Speaking words in Spanish is easier than it is in the English language. That's mainly because if you see a letter in Spanish, you will understand how to speak the sound of that particular letter. The only difficult part of the pronunciation of the Spanish language is that you will find sounds in the language, which do not exist, in the English language. All of them could be hard to speak at first.

Every vowel – **a, e, i, o, u** – make only one sound in Spanish. It is only a quick sound, which remains the same from start to finish,

Here's a detailed example:

- The vowel **A** seen in the typical Spanish term **casa** is the simplest vowel sound to create. The other four vowel sounds concentrate on maintaining the vowel sound brief and constant.
- The vowel **E** creates the sound spoken in the English word "t<u>a</u>ke." You see, it is not pronounced "eyyyy." You do not end it off at the end as we mostly do in the English language.
- The vowel **I** create the sound spoken in the word "f<u>ee</u>." It is not "iyyy."
- The vowel **B** creates the sound spoken in "t<u>o</u>il." It is not "owww."
- The vowel **U** creates the sound spoken in "r<u>u</u>le." It is not "uwww."

D. Pronunciation

Pronunciation is vital in any type of language. Therefore, get the hang of this before you try to talk to someone. Nowadays, it is much simpler, simply because you will find countless videos online that will aid you. In this section, you will learn how to utter individual letters by fitting them into typical, easily spoken Spanish words. One benefits of Spanish over the English language is that with the majority of words, the pronunciation is phonetic. You see, the words sound as if they're spelled. You will also find some homophones that will puzzle you. Some of those words include "they're," "their," and "there" that sound the same; however, have different spellings and meanings. Below is a brief guide to Spanish pronunciation.

The Vowels

In the Spanish language, you will find five vowels and one sound for every vowel.

[a]	ah	The 'a' is spoken as if you were gargling. Simply open your mouth wide and say as saw and father. Try **mapa, agua.**
[e]	eh	The 'e' sound isn't totally existent in English. The nearest pronunciation might be 'eh' as red and met. You must not say the 'e' as in English. You can try saying **enero, verde.**
[i]	ee	The 'i' sound is somewhat similar to 'ee' as bee and feet. You see, the 'i' sound is much different compared to the English pronunciation. For instance, **mi, fino.**
[o]	oh	The letter 'o' is uttered as 'oh.' However, it has a shorter sound as know and boat. You can try **roto, coco.**

| [u] | oo | This is pronounced as 'oo' like in do or boot. Try saying **muro, futuro**. |

The Diphthongs

In case you didn't know yet, a diphthong is a sound that was made by a mix of two (2) vowels in a single syllable. A sound starts as one vowel and moves to another.

|a|+|i|	ai, ay	The 'ai' and 'ay' sound is like ay and why. You can try speaking **mayo, aire.**
|a|+|u|	au	The 'au' sounds like the expression auch. You can try speaking **aula, aunque.**
|e|+|u|	eu	You will not find a sound for this in the English language. That was something like ew however, with the use of the 'e' sound as bed and the 'u' as do. You can try saying **deudor, Europa.**
|e|+|i|	ey, ei	The pronunciation of 'ey' and ei' is near to say and hey. Try saying **buy, reina.**
|i|+|a|	ia	The 'ia' will sounds like tiara and yah. Try saying **anciano, piano.**
|i|+|e|	ie	The 'ic' sounds similar to yes. Try saying **fiera, tierra.**
|i|+|o|	io	The 'io' is uttered as John or yo-yo. Try saying **rio, radio.**
|i|+|u|	iu	The 'iu' is uttered as you. You can try saying **viuda, ciudad.**
|o|+|i|	oy, oi	The 'oy' and 'oi' sounds similar to boy and toy. Try saying **heroico, hoy.**
|u|+|a|	ua	The 'ua' sound is similar to water. You can try saying **aduana, actuar.**
|u|+|e|	ue	The 'ue' sounds similar to wet. Try saying **sueño** and **Huevo**.
u|+|i|	ui	The 'ui' sounds is similar to wheat and we. Try saying **huir, arruinar.**
|u|+|o|	uo	The 'uo' sounds similar to continuous and quote. Try saying **cuota, individuo.**

The Consonants

A series of Spanish consonants are pronounced differently from their English counterparts. If you could, you can try to listen to a local speaker and hear how they deal with them.

[b]	beh	The letter 'b' is uttered after n, m, or l. The sound of this letter is similar to bear and Venice, even though the lips should not touch. For example, **bonito.**
[c]	ceh	The letter 'c' sounds like cereal before i or e. Or else, it might sound like 'k' as computer. For example, **computadora** as 'k' and **cereza** as 'c.'
[ch]	cheh	For example, **chico, chocolate.**
[d]	deh	For example, **dos, dust.**
[f]	effe	The letter 'f' sounds similar in the English fountain or Eiffel. For example, **familia.**
[g]	heh	The 'g' sounds is similar to her before i or e. Or else, it sounds like get or got. For example, **guante** as 'get,' **gesto** as 'her.'
[h]	hache	The letter 'h' in Spanish is silent. For example, **hilo.**
[j]	hotah	The letter 'j' sounds harsh or horse. But never as jump or jar. For example, **jirafa.**
[k]	kah	The letter 'k' sounds similar as in the English language. It is pronounced as key or car. For example, **koala.**
[l]	ele	The letter 'l' is uttered as like or lord. For example, **lobo.**
[ll]	double ele, elle	The double 'l' is spoken as the 'y' in yesterday. For example, **calle.**
[m]	emeh	The letter 'm' is similar as in the English man or mother. For example, **modo.**
[n]	eneh	The letter 'n' sounds similar as in the English note and no. For example, **nosotros.**
[ń|	enyeh	The 'ń' isn't another letter 'n'. This letter sounds as canyon, onion or lasagna. For example, **nińa.**
[p]	peh	The letter 'p' is similar to the sound in the English paste or pet. For example, **pelo.**
[q]	koo	The letter 'q' is spoken as curious. If it is written with 'ue' and 'ui' the letter 'u' is silent. For instance, '¿quién?' is

		spoken as *kien*. What's more, the '¿qué?' as *ke* (using the Spanish 'e'). For example, **qué, quién.**
[r]	ere	The letter 'r' sounds like brr at the start of a word. Or else, it sounds like brown or break. For example, **raton** as 'brr,' **crear** as 'break.'
[rr]	erre	The double 'r' sounds like 'r' at the start of a word. It is sound is much vibrated, as the sound of a vehicle accelerating. For example, **perro.**
[s]	ese	The letter 's' sounds similarly as in the English language sea or sorry. For example, **solo.**
[sh]	esse / hache	The 'sh' sounds as show or shampoo. For example, **show.**
[t]	teh	The 't' sound is pronounced as in English, even though the tongue needs to touch the back of your teeth like test and tea. For example, **tela.**
[v]	veh	The 'v' sounds are proncounced as the letter 'b.' However, your lips are touched slightly as voice or various. For example, **vecino.**
[w]	doble veh	The 'w' sounds have a similar pronunciation as in the English language wine and whiskey. For example, **kiwi.**
[x]	equis	The 'x' sound is spoken as 'gs' or 'ks' like in excited or explosion. For example, **xilófono.**
[y]	i griega / ye	The letter 'y' is the same as the double 'l.' However, it has a slight difference as yellow and crayon. For example, **yegua.**
[z]	setah	The letter 'z' is uttered as 'th' not as in zero or zip. For example, **zorro.**

Are you now looking for ways to make it simpler for you to say these letters as a native Spanish speaker? Then there's no need for you to worry. You could look online for an audio file and listen to it to make sure you get it all right.

We suggest that you stay away from any translation software when learning how to pronounce any word in the Spanish language. The reason behind this is that such applications do not have the required accent to make you pronounce each word accurately.

Make sure you look for real individuals speaking in the native Spanish language on different video platforms. These people tend to speak authentic Spanish, meaning you could learn more from them and much quicker.

E.   Where to Go From Here

The best thing about this book is that you don't need to read them every chapter from the start to the end. Every chapter stands on its own, and it does not oblige you to finish any other of the chapters within the book. That setup saves you sufficient time if you have mastered particular topics but feel somewhat insecure about the others.

Therefore, make sure you leap right in. Now is a perfect time that you get your feet wet. If you not certain exactly where to start, you can look at the Table of Contents. Choose the topic, which appears to best suit your requirements and capabilities. If you are getting concerned that your existing background might not be strong enough, you could begin at the very start. From them, you could work way throughout the book.

Just bear in mind that learning the Spanish language is not a sort of competition. You must work at a pace, which fits your needs. Do not pause to read a chapter a second, third, or even fifth time many days later. Take note that you could adapt this book easily into your learning skills. You need to take note that you should have a positive and confident outlook towards this.

Indeed, you will make some mistakes. Everybody does – in fact; most native Spanish speakers always do. Your goal here is to speak and write. If you could make yourself understood, you have won the greatest part of the war.

F.   The Stress Rules

You are already aware that Spanish words are stressed on the *last syllable* when they end in a consonant other than s or n. For example, **Gibraltar, Santander, El Escorial, Valladolild.**

You see, they are stressed on the *syllable before last* when they end in s or n or a vowel. For example, **Valdepeñas, Toledo, Granada.**

When a particular word breaks either of such rules, an accent is written to highlight where the stress falls. For example **civilización, José, Gifón, kilómetro, Cádiz, Málaga.** Every word ending in –ion bears that accent. Therefore, if you notice a written accent, you should stress the syllable where the accent is located. The only other usage of accents you must understand is that it is situated on *si* to distinguish **si** (yes) from **si** (if).

The only other usage of accents you must understand is that it is situated on *si* to distinguish **si** (yes) from **si** (if).

OTHER IMPORTANT LESSONS TO LEARN ABOUT SPANISH LANGUAGE

(OTRAS LECCIONES IMPORTANTES PARA APRENDER SOBRE LENGUA ESPAÑOL)

A. TIME *(HORA)*

If you are working in an Office or Establishment, then the customers there are of varied nationalities, and surely these customers will ask you about anything under the sun. How about, if he asks you about the time, what will you do in return or in exchange of the services? *(Si está trabajando en una oficina o establecimiento, entonces los clientes allí son de variadas nacionalidades, y seguramente estos clientes le preguntarán acerca de cualquier cosa bajo el sol. ¿Qué tal si le pregunta sobre la hora, qué hará a cambio o a cambio de los servicios?)*

TIME IN ENGLISH *(Tiempo en Ingles)*	SPANISH EQUIVALENT *(Equivalente Español)*
One o'clock; 1:00	La una en punto
Two o'clock; 2:00	Dos en punto
Three o'clock; 3:00	Tres en punto
Four o'clock; 4:00	Cuatro en punto
Five o'clock; 5:00	Cinco en punto
Six o'clock; 6:00	Seis en punto
Seven o'clock; 7:00	Siete en punto
Eight o'clock; 8:00	Otso en piunto
Nine o'clock; 9:00	Nueve en punto
Ten o'clock; 10:00	Diez en punto
Eleven o'clock; 11:00	Onse en punto
Twelve o'clock; 12:00	Dose en punto

B. ADJECTIVES
(ADJETIVO/A)

You are familiar with the definition of the adjective as that particular word describing a person, place, thing or an event which is the subject of the sentence. The following are known as the most common adjectives used in the Spanish Language: (*Usted está familiarizado con la definición de adjetivo como esa palabra en particular que describe a una persona, lugar, cosa o evento que es el sujeto de la oración.*

Los siguientes son los adjetivos más comunes utilizados en el idioma español:)

ENGLISH ADJECTIVE (INGLÉS ADJETIVO)	SPANISH EQUIVALENT (EQUIVALENTE ESPAÑOL)
Beautiful	Hermoso/a
Kind	Tipo
Caring	Cuidando
Thoughtful	Pensativo/a
Wonderful	Maravilloso/a
Happy	Feliz
Inspiring	Inspirador/a

C. ADVERBS
(ADVERBIO)

If an adjective is describing a noun which is the subject of the sentence, then the adverb is describing a verb. There are three kinds of adverb, and you should know about this because it will help you a lot in your journey towards learning the Spanish Language. *(Si un adjetivo está describiendo un sustantivo que es el sujeto de la oración, entonces el adverbio está describiendo un verbo. Hay tres tipos de adverbio y debes saberlo porque te ayudará mucho en tu viaje hacia el aprendizaje del idioma español.)*

Adverbs of Manner *Adverbio de Modo*	Adverbs of Frequency *Adverbio de frecuencia*	Adverbs of Place *Adverbio de Lugar*	Adverbs of Time *Adverbio de Tiempo*
This is the kind of adverb which describes how a particular thing or event is done. *Este es el tipo de adverbio que describe cómo se hace una cosa o evento en particular.*	This is the kind of adverb which describes how fast or how often the event does transpire. *Este es el tipo de adverbio que describe qué tan rápido o con qué frecuencia se produce el evento.*	This is the kind of adverb that describes where an action took place. *Este es el tipo de adverbio que describe dónde tuvo lugar una acción*	This is the kind of adverb that describes when or what times an action took place. *Este es el tipo de adverbio que describe cuándo o en qué momento*

			tuvo lugar una acción.

D. PREPOSITIONS
(PREPOSICION)

To some, the preposition is a very scary thing to learn. However, that is not true. The preposition is just a word that connected two elements composing a sentence. *(Para algunos, la preposición es algo muy aterrador de aprender. Sin embargo, eso no es cierto. La preposición es solo una palabra que conecta dos elementos que componen una oración.)*

For example, the following phrases or combination of words are **prepositions:**

ENGLISH PREPOSITION *(PREPOSICION INGLESA)*	SPANISH PREPOSITION *(PREPOSICION ESPAÑOLA)*
1. Caja De Chocolates	Box of Chocolates
2. Bolsa De Dulces	Bag of Candies
3. Banco De Dinero	Bank of Money

E. NOUNS
(SUSTANTIVOS)

Just like the English Alphabet, a *noun* is either the subject or the object of the sentence. The noun may be used either way, as in these examples: *(Al igual que el alfabeto inglés, un sustantivo es el sujeto o el objeto de la oración. El sustantivo se puede usar de cualquier manera, como en estos ejemplos:)*

SUBJECT NOUN/ *SUSTANTIVO*	OBJECT NOUN/ *NOMBRE DEL OBJETO*
The **bag** is red.	That thing which is colored red is a **bag**.

In which case, both **bag** is considered as a noun, either as subject or as an object. *(En cuyo caso, ambas bolsas se consideran como un sustantivo, ya sea como sujeto o como un objeto.)*

VERBS

(VERBOS)

A. CONJUGATION OF VERBS
(CONJUGACIÓN DE VERBOS)

Even in other languages, a verb is a part of a speech that denotes an action or a state of being. In Spanish like in English, verbs can be in an infinitive form. They are called conjugated in Spanish. The function of a conjugated verb is to show the state of the action. Infinitives in Spanish, infinitives can have three different endings, namely –ar, -er and –ir. *(Incluso en otros idiomas, un verbo es parte de un discurso que denota una acción o un estado de ser. En español como en inglés, los verbos pueden estar en forma infinitiva. Se llaman conjugados en español. La función de un verbo conjugado es mostrar el estado de la acción. Infinitivos en español, los infinitivos pueden tener tres terminaciones diferentes: –ar, -er y –ir.)*
Here is a sample conjugation of the verb to swim:
(Aquí hay una muestra de conjugación del verbo nadar:)

nadar (to swim)
Le gusta nadar. (He likes to swim.)
Basically, the infinitive form of the verb has two parts: the stem of the word (which is everything before the ending) and the ending itself (which is either -ar, -er, or -ir). For example, the stem of viajar ("to travel") is viaj-, and the verb's ending is -ar. Once you've identified the stem of a verb, you conjugate the verb by adding the appropriate ending to the stem for the given subject. *(Básicamente, la forma infinitiva del verbo tiene dos partes: la raíz de la palabra (que es todo antes de la terminación) y la terminación misma (que es -ar, -er o -ir). Por ejemplo, la raíz de viajar ("viajar") es viaj-, y la terminación del verbo es -ar. Una vez que ha identificado la raíz de un verbo, conjuga el verbo agregando la terminación apropiada a la raíz del tema dado.)*
The importance of conjugating verbs is it tells whether the action was, is or will be and also when and by whom. *(La importancia de conjugar verbos es si indica si la acción fue, es o será y también cuándo y por quién.*

Verb Vocabulary (Vocabulario Verbo)

abrazar - to hug, to embrace

abrir - to open

abrochar - to fasten, to button up, to do up, to buckle

aburrirse - to get bored

abusar - to abuse, to take advantage of

acabar - to finish, to end

acariciar - to caress, to stroke

aceptar - to accept, to agree

acercar - to get closer

aclarar- to clarify, to clear up

acordar - to remember, to agree

acostarse- to lie down, to go to bed

actuar - to act

acudir - to go, to come, to turn to

acusar - to accuse, to charge

adivinar- to guess

administrar - to manage, to administer

admirar - to admire, to amaze

admitir - to admit, to allow entry

adorar - to adore, to love, to worship

afeitarse - to shave

aguantar - to bear, to endure, to tolerate

ahorrar - to save, to spare

alcanzar - to reach, to catch, to achieve, to be sufficient

alegrarse - to be glad, to be happy

aliviarse - to get better, to be relieved

alquilar- to rent, to lease, to hire

amar - to love

amarrar- to tie, to moor

analizar- to analyze

andar- to walk, to go ahead, to work

apagar- to turn off, to switch off

aplicar- to apply, to put into practice

apoyar- to support, to back

apreciar- to be fond of to appreciate, to see

aprender - to learn

aprobar - to approve, to pass (an exam)

aprovechar - to make the most of, to use

armar - to assemble, to put together, to arm

arreglar - to fix, to repair, to arrange, to sort out

asistir - to attend, to assist

asolearse - to sunbathe

atar - to tie

atender - to pay attention, to serve, to tend to

aterrizar - to land, to arrive

atrapar - to catch

atravesar - to cross, to go through

auxiliar - to help, to assist

aventar - to throw

averiguar- to find out

avisar - to notify to warn, to let know

ayudar- to help

bailar - to dance

bajar - to go down, to come down, to lower, to download

banarse - to take a bath

barrer - to sweep, to sweep awayt

batallar - to battle, to fight, to struggle

batir - to beat, to churn, to mix

beber- to drink

besar - to kiss

borrar - to delete, to erase, to clear

bostezar- to yawn

brincar - to jump, to skip

bucear- to dive

buscar- to look for, to search

caber - to fit, to hold (capacity)

caer - to fall

callarse - to be quiet, to shut up

calmarse - to calm down, to ease off

cambiar- to change, to swap

caminar-. to walk

cansarse - to get tired

cantar - to sing

captar - to attract, to grasp, to get, to gain

carecer - to lack, to be lacking

cargar -to load, to bear, to charge, to fuel, to carry

casarse - to get married

castigar- to punish, to penalize

cazar - to hunt

celebrar- to celebrate, to perform

cenar- to have dinner

cepillar - to brush, to plane (wood)

cerrar - to close, to shut, to turn off

checar- to check

chiflar - to whistle, to boo

chocar- to crash, to collide, to run, into

cobrar - to charge, to earn, to cash, to collect

cocer - to cook, to boil, to bake

cocinar - to cook

coger - to take, to pick, to catch, to get

cojear - to limp, to hobble, to wobble

colaborar- to collaborate, to cooperate

coleccionar - to collect

colgar - to hang, to put up

colocar - to place, to put, to lay

comenzar- to begin, to start

comer - to eat

cometer - to commit, to make

comparar- to compare

compartir - to share

componer - to fix, to repair, to compose

comportarse - to behave

comprar - to buy, to purchase, to bribe

comprender - to understand, to comprehend, to included, to cover

concordar - to agree, to concur

conducir - to drive

conectar - to connect, to link

confesar - to confess, to admit

confiar- to trust, to be confident

confirmar- to confirm

conjugar - to conjugate, to combine

conocer- to know, to meet

conseguir - to get, to obtain, to achieve

conservar - to keep, to preserve

considerer- to consider, to take into account

construir - to build, to construct

consumir- to consume

contagiarse - to get infected

contar - to count, to tell

contestar - to answer, to reply

continuar- to continue, to go on

contribuir - to contribute

controlar - to control

convencer - to convince, to persuade

conversar - to talk, to chat

copiar - to copy, to imitate, to cheat

coquetear - to flirt

corregir - to correct, to grade

correr - to run

cortar - to cut, to chop, to break up

crear - to create

crecer - to grow, to rise

creer - to believe, to think

criticar - to criticize, to review

cruzar - to cross, to go across

cuidar - to take care, to look after

culpar - to blame, to accuse

cumplir - to fulfill, to accomplish, to carry out, to turn (age)

curar - to cure, to heal

danar- to damage, to harm

dar - to give

deber- to owe, to have to, must, should

decidir - to decide

decir - to tell, to say

declarar- to declare, to state, to aunounce, to testify

deducir - to deduce, to deduct

dejar - to leave, to abaudou, to let, to stop doing something

demostrar - to demonstrate, to show, to prove

derramar - to spill, to shed

derribar- to demolish, to knock down, to bring down

desaparecer - to disappear, to vanish

desarmar - to dismantle, to disarm, to take apart

desarrollar - to develop

desatar - to untie, to uudo, to unleash

desayunar - to have breakfast

descansar - to rest

descender - to descend, to fall, to go down

describir - to describe

descubrir- to discover, to find out, to uncover, to reveal

descuidar - to neglect, to be inattentive

desear- to wish, to desire, to want

desesperarse - to despair, to get exasperated

desfallecer - to faint, to feel faint, to lose heart

desgarrar- to tear, to rip

deshacer - to undo, to untie, to break up

desmayarse - to faint

despedirse - to say good-bye

desperdiciar - to waste

despertar- to wake, to awaken, to arouse

despreciar - to look down on, to despise, to reject

destapar - to unblock, to open, to take a lid off

destruir - to destroy, to ruin, to wreck

desvelarse - to stay awake

detener - to stop, to halt, to detain, to arrest

detestar - to detest, to hate

devolver - to give back, to return, to throw up

dibujar - to draw, to sketch

dirigir - to run, to manage, to direct

disculpar - to excuse, to forgive

discutir - to argue, to discuss, to debate

disfrazarse - to dress up

disfrutar - to enjoy to have a good time

disponer - to stipulate, to order, to arrange, to have available

distinguir - to distiuguish, to make out, to honor

divertirse - to have fun, to have a good time, to enjoy oneself

doblar - to fold, to turn, to dub

dormir - to sleep

dudar - to doubt, to hesitate

echar - to throw, to expel, to put

elaborar - to produce, to make, to develop, to prepare

elegir - to choose, to elect

elevar - to raise, to lift, to increase

eliminar - to eliminate, to get rid of to remove

embarcarse - to board, to go on board, to undertake

emborracharse - to get drunk

emocionarse - to get excited, to be moved, to get upset

empatar - to tie, to get even, to match

empezar - to start, to begin

emplear - to employ, to use

emprender - to undertake, to embark on, to set out

empujar - to push, to shove, to drive

enamorarse - to fall in love

encargar - to ask, to order, to take care

encender- to light, to switch on, to awaken

enchufar - to plug in, to switch on, to set up with

encontrar- to find

enderezar - to straighten, to sort out

endulzar - to sweeten, to soften, to brighten up

enfermarse - to fall ill, to get ill, to get sick

enflacar - to lose weight, to get thin

enganar - to deceive, to mislead, to cheat on

engordar - to put on or gain weight, to fatten, to swell

enloquecer - to go crazy, to drive iusane, to be mad about

enojarse - to get angry, to get mad

ensayar - to rehearse, to try, to test, to practice

ensenar - to teach, to show

ensuciar - to get dirty, to sully

entender - to understand, to know

entrar - to enter, to go or come in, to start

entregar - to deliver, to give, to turn in

entrenarse - to train

entristecerse - to grow sad, to become sad

enviar - to send, to dispatch

equivocarse - to make a mistake, to be wrong

escalar - to climb, to scale

escapar - to escape, to run away, to get away

escoger - to choose, to pick, to select

esconder - to hide

escribir - to write

escuchar - to listen, to hear

esperar - to wait, to expect, to hope

estar - to be

estornudar - to sneeze

estudiar - to study, to learn, to consider

evitar - to avoid, to prevent, to save

examinar- to examine, to inspect, to study

explicar - to explain

explorar - to explore, to examine, to scout, to surf (Web)

expresar - to express, to state

extraviar - to lose, to misplace

fabricar - to manufacture, to produce, to make

fallar - to fail, to go wrong, to miss, to rule (legal)

faltar - to miss, to need, to lack

fingir - to feigu, to pretend

fracasar - to fail, to be unsuccessful

frenar - to brake, to stop, to slow down

fumar - to smoke

ganar - to earn, to win, to gain

gastar - to spend, to waste

girar - to turn, to spin, to revolve

gobernar - to govern, to rule

golpear - to hit, to beat

gozar - to enjoy to have fun, to take pleasure

grabar - to record, to engrave, to etch

gritar - to shout, to scream, to yell

guardar - to keep, to put away, to save

habitar - to live in, to dwell

hablar - to speak, to talk

hacer - to do, to make

hallar - to find

heredar - to inherit, to succeed to, to get from

herir - to hurt, to wound

hervir - to boil

hoxnear - to balce

huir - to escape, to run away, to avoid something

ignorar - to ignore, to be unaware of

imaginar - to imagine

imitar - to imitate, to simulate, to copy

impeder - to prevent, to hinder, to impede

imprimir - to print

indicar - to indicate, to show

ingresar - to join, to enter, to be admitted, to deposit

iniciar - to begin, to start, to initiate

insistir - to insist

intentar - to try, to attempt

interferir - to interfere, to meddle

intuir - to sense, to intuit, to have a feeling

inventar - to invent, to come up with, to make up

invertir - to invest, to reverse

investigar - to investigate, to find out, to do research

invitar - to invite, to treat

ir - to go

jalar - to pull, to flush

jugar - to play

juntar - to put together, to join, to collect, to unite

jurar - to swear (an oath)

juzgar - to judge, to consider

laborar - to work, to labor

lamentar - to regret, to be sorry

lanzar - to throw, to launch

lastimar - to hurt

lavar - to wash, to clean

leer - to read

levantar - to lift, to raise

limpiar - to clean, to clear

llamar - to call, to summon, to phone, to knock

llegar - to arrive, to reach, to come

llenar - to fill

llevar- to take, to wear, to carry

llorar - to cry

lograr - to achieve, to attain, to manage

luchar - to struggle, to fight

madrugar- to get up early

mandar - to command, to order, to send

manejar - to handle, to drive, to manipulate

maquillarse - to put on makeup

masticar - to chew

matar - to kill

memorizar - to memorize

mentir - to lie

merecer - to deserve

merendar - to have an afternoon snack, to have an early diner

meter - to put in

mezclar - to mix

mirar - to look, to watch

molestar - to disturb, to bother, to upset

montar- to ride

morar - to dwell, to reside

morder - to bite

morir - to die

mostrar - to show, to display

mover - to move, to drive

mudarse - to move (dwelling), to change (clothes)

nacer - to be born

nadar - to swim

narrar - to tell, to narrate, to relate

necesitar - to need, to require

negar - to deny, to refuse

nombrar - to name, to mention, to appoint

notar - to notice, to note

obedecer - to obey, to respond

obligar- to force, to require

observar - to observe, to watch

obtener - to obtain, to get

ocultar- to hide, to conceal

odiar - to hate

ofrecer- to offer

ofr - to hear, to listen

oler - to smell

olvidar- to forget

omitir - to omit, to leave out

opinar - to express an opinion, to think

oponerse - to be opposed, to object

ordenar - to arrange, to tidy up, to order, to ordain

organizar- to organize, to arrange

osar - to dare

padecer- to suffer, to endure

pagar - to pay

parar - to stop

parecerse - to be alike, to look like, to resemble

participar - to take part, to participate, to announce

pasar- to pass, to go past, to go by, to cross, to happen

pasear - to take a walk (a stroll, a ride)

patear - to kick

pedir - to ask for, to order, to beg

pegar - to hit, to stick, to glue, to paste

pelear - to fight, to quarrel

pensar- to think

percibir - to perceive, to sense, to receive

perder- to lose

perdonar - to forgive, to excuse

perjudicar - to harm, to be detrimental, to damage

permitir - to allow, to permit, to make possible

perseguir- to chase, to pursue

perseverar - to persevere, to persist

pintar - to paint

planear - to plan

poder - to be able to, can, may

poner - to put, to set, to set up, to turn on

poseer - to possess, to own, to have

practicar - to practice, to play, to perform

preferir - to prefer

preguntar - to ask

prender - to turn on, to light, to pin, to catch

preocuparse - to worry, to be concerned

preparar - to prepare, to make

presenter - to present, to introduce

prestart - to lend

presumir - to boast, to predict, to suppose

pretender - to expect, to aspire, to pretend

principiar - to begin, to start

probar - to prove, to try, to test, to taste

procurar - to try, to get

prohibir - to prohibit, to ban, to forbid

prometer - to promise, to be promising

pronunciar - to pronounce, to give (a speech)

proponer - to propose, to suggest

proseguir - to continue, to carry on

proteger - to protect

protestar - to protest, to complain

proveer - to provide, to supply

quedarse - to stay, to remain

querer- to want, to love

quitar - to remove, to take away, to get out

rascar - to scratch

rechazar - to reject, to turn down, to repel

recibir- to receive, to get, to welcome

reciclar - to recycle

reclamar - to demand, to claim, to complain

recobrar - to recover, to retrieve, to regain

recoger - to pick up, to collect, to tidy up

reconocer - to recognize, to admit, to reconnoiter

recordar - to recall, to remember, to remind

reflexionar - to reflect, to think

regalar- to present (as a gift), to give away

regañar - to scold, to give a talking to

regir - to rule, to manage, to control

regresar - to return, to go back, to give back

rehusar - to refuse

reír - to laugh

relajarse - to relax, to slacken

remplazar - to replace, to substitute

rendirse - to surrender, to give up, to bow

rentar - to rent, to lease, to yield

renunciar - to resign, to quit, to renounce

reparar - to repair, to fix, to correct, to notice

repartir - to allocate, to distribute, to hand out

repasar - to review, to check, to go over

reponer - to replace, to put back

representar - to represent, to signify, to symbolize, to perform

rescatar - to rescue, to save, to recover

reservar - to reserve

resguardar - to safeguard, to protect

resistir- to resist, to stand, to bear

resolver - to solve, to resolve, to settle, to decide

respetar - to respect, to obey

respirar - to breathe

responder - to answer, to reply, to respond

retroceder - to move back, to back away, to back down

reunirse - to meet, to reunite

revisar - to inspect, to check, to review

revolver - to stir, to mix, to agitate

rezar - to pray, to say

rogar - to beg, to request, to pray

romper - to break, to smash, to tear

roncar - to snore

saber - to know, to know how

sacar - to take out, to get, to take (a picture)

salir - to go out, to get out, to leave, to date

saltar - to jump, to leap, to bounce

saludar - to greet, to say hello, to salute

seguir - to follow, to continue, to keep on

sentarse - to sit

sentir - to feel, to be sorry, to regret, to hear

ser - to be

server - to serve, to be of use for

situar - to locate, to set, to post

sobrevivir - to survive

socorrer - to help, to aid

solicitar - to request, to apply for

soltar - to let go, to release

solucionar - to solve, to resolve

sonar - to dream

soportar - to support, to bear, to stand

sospechar - to suspect

sostener - to support, to hold, to uphold, to maintain

subir - to go up, to climb, to raise

sudar - to sweat

sufrir - to suffer, to bear, put up with

---

sugerir - to suggest, to recommend, to propose

suicidarse - to commit suicide, to kill oneself

suplicar - to implore, to beg, to beseech

suponer - to suppose, to assume, to involve

suspirar - to sigh

susurrar – to whisper, to murmur

tapar - to cover, to put the lid (cap, cover) on, to block

tardar - to take (a long) time

teclear - to key, to type

tejer - to knit, to weave

temblar - to tremble, to shake, to shiver, to shudder

temer - to fear, to dread, to be afraid

tener - to have, to hold, to be (age, measure, condition)

terminar - to end, to end up, to finish

tirar - to throw, to toss, to throw away, to drop

tocar - to touch, to handle, to play (a musical instrument)

tomar - to take, to drink

trabajar - to work

traducir - to translate

traer - to bring, to cause, to wear

transportar - to transport, to carry

tratar - to treat, to try to, to deal with

trepar - to climb, to creep up

tropezar - to trip, to stumble, to run into

usar - to use, to wear

utilizar - to use, to utilize

vencer - to defeat, to overcome, to expire

vender- to sell, to sell out, to betray

venir - to come

ver - to see, to look

vestir - to dress, to clothe, to wear

viajar- to travel, to journey

vigilar - to watch, to keep an eye on, to guard

visitar - to visit

vivir - to live, to make a living

volar - to fly

voltear - to turn over, to turn, to toss

volver - to return, to come / go back, to do again

vomitar - to vomit, to throw up, to spew out

votar - to vote

yacer - to lie (dead)

zarpar - to set sail, to weigh anchor

B. AS IF: CONDITIONAL TENSE

(COMO SI: TIEMPO CONDICIONAL)

As if's are theoretical. They are the "conditionally appropriate" without the assurance that they will happen. In English, they come in forms of "I would've if. . ." Basically, conditional tense is laid out for a conditional action. You can also make it as a request to show that somebody can do the particular action. *(Cuando los ifs son teóricos. Ellos son el con reservas apropiados sin el aseguramiento que ellos pasarán. En Inglés, ellos vienen a formas "de yo tendría si..." Básicamente, el tiempo condicional es presentado para una acción condicional. Usted también puede hacerlo como una petición para mostrar que alguien puede hacer la acción particular.)*

In the following sentences, observe how the regular and irregular conditions of the conditional tense are formed. You will find out how to form the conditional tense and how to utilize it in a sentence. *(En las oraciones siguientes, observe como las condiciones regulares e irregulares del tiempo condicional son formadas. Usted averiguará como formar el tiempo condicional y como utilizarlo en una oración.)*

WAFFLING WITH THE CONDITIONAL TENSE

The conditional tense can be used if you are waffling on issues. You could be able to state an impossible action or set of conditions you like and then say you would've done something if only that condition or set of conditions had been in place. It can be stated in every language either English, Spanish or Italian or any other else. You do not have to be a politician to use it. *(El tiempo condicional puede ser usado si usted es waffling en cuestiones. Usted puede ser capaz de declarar una acción imposible o ponerse de condiciones que le gustan y luego dice que usted habría hecho algo si sólo que la condición o se puso de condiciones hubiera estado en el lugar. Puede ser declarado en cada lengua inglés, español o italiano o alguno otro más. Usted no tiene que ser un político para usarlo.)*

Usually, the conditional tense is used in a sentence with two verbs. One verb states the condition or problem, and then the second verb states, in the conditional, what you would personally do if you were faced with the same problem. For example, in the sentence, "If only I had been given another chance at love, I would try to be the better person," the first verb states what situation you are in and in the second, what you would do if you are in the situation. *(Por lo general, el tiempo condicional es usado en una oración con dos verbos. Un verbo declara la condición o el problema, y luego los segundos estados de verbo, en el condicional, lo que usted haría personalmente si usted fuera afrontado con el mismo problema. Por ejemplo, en la oración, "Si sólo me hubieran dado otra posibilidad en el amor, trataré de ser la mejor persona," el primer verbo declara que situación usted está en y en el segundo, lo que usted haría si usted está en la situación.)*

REGULAR CONDITIONALS

In English, the main word in forming the conditional tense is would. You or somebody else will certainly do these things if the conditions are arguably just. In Spanish, however, you actually change the form of the verb to build the sense of would right into it. Whenever conjugating Spanish verbs in the regular conditional tense, remember the following points *(En Inglés, la palabra principal en la formación del tiempo condicional es. Usted o alguien más harían ciertamente estas cosas si las condiciones son posiblemente sólo. En Español, sin embargo, usted realmente se cambia la forma del verbo para construir el sentido de directamente en ello. Conjugando verbos españoles en el tiempo condicional regular, recuerde los puntos siguientes)*:

The regular conditional tense is a combination of the imperfect and future tenses. It requires no spelling or stem changes.When conjugating regular -ar, -er, and -ir verbs in the conditional tense, you simply take the entire verb infinitive (don't drop anything) and then add the imperfect verb endings you use for -er and -ir verbs. *(El tiempo condicional regular es una combinación del imperfecto y futuros. Esto no requiere ninguna ortografía o cambios de tallo. Conjugando-ar regular,-er, y verbos-ir en el tiempo condicional, usted simplemente toma el infinitivo de verbo entero (no deje caer nada) y luego añada los finales de verbo imperfectos que usted usa para-er y verbos-ir.)*

Consider the following examples (Considere los ejemplos siguientes):

Conditional endings for all verbs

yo –ía	nosotros/as -íamos
tú –ías	vosotros/as -íais
él, ella, usted –ía	ellos/as, ustedes –ían

Here is a table for conjugations of the following verb types (*Aquí está una mesa para conjugaciones de los tipos de verbo siguientes*):

preparar (to prepare)

prepararía	prepararíamos
prepararías	prepararíais
prepararía	prepararían

Ud. prepararía. (You [formal] would prepare.)

vender (to sell)

vendería	venderíamos
prepararías	venderíais
venderías	venderían

Vosotras venderíais. (You [informal, plural, female] would sell.)

escribir (to write)

escribiría	escribiríamos
escribirías	escribiríais
escribiría	escribirían

Ella escribiría. (She would write.)

C. INDICATIVE VS. SUBJUNCTIVE (*INDICATIVO VS. SUBJUNTIVO*)

When it comes to verbal moods, think of two separate timelines that are running parallel to each other. The indicative mood is one where things have actually happened in the past, are happening in the present and will happen in the future. Meanwhile, the other timeline is called subjunctive. It is where things may or may not happen or may or may not have happened – like desires. The subjunctive mood is a plethora of uncertainties, while the indicative one is always grounded in reality. In practice, a subjunctive clause always depends, at least implicitly, on an indicative statement; they are linked by a conjunctive element, most often "que." *(Cuando esto viene a humores verbales, piense en dos objetivos separados que dirigen la paralela el uno al otro. El humor indicativo es el que donde las cosas realmente han pasado en el pasado, pasan en el presente y pasarán en lo venidero. Mientras tanto, el otro objetivo es llamado el subjuntivo. Es donde las cosas pueden o poder no pasar o puede o poder no haber pasado – como deseos. El modo subjuntivo es muchas incertidumbres mientras el indicativo siempre es basado en realidad. En la práctica, una cláusula subjuntiva siempre depende, al menos implícitamente, en una declaración indicativa; ellos son unidos por un elemento conjuntivo, el más a menudo "que.")*

Consider the following example:

> Es posible que vaya a México en verano. (It is possible that I will go to Mexico in the summer.)

Generally speaking, the subjunctive is used to converse about situations that go beyond the control of a sentence's primary subject. It is outcome is mostly uncertain. It is more like a wish. One example of this is when we expect drivers to arrive at a full stop in stop signs, but it does not necessarily mean that they will. We wish for it to happen, but it depends still. It is the same way as Teresita wanting to lend the money to Pedring, but there is still a possibility that Pedro will refuse. *(Hablando en general, el subjuntivo está acostumbrado opuesto sobre situaciones que van más allá del control del sujeto primario de una oración. Esto es el resultado es sobre todo incierto. Es más bien un deseo. Un ejemplo de este es cuando esperamos que choferes lleguen a un punto en signos de parada pero esto no necesariamente significa que ellos van a. Deseamos para ello pasar pero esto depende todavía. Esto es el mismo camino que Teresita deseo para prestar el dinero a Pedring, pero hay todavía una posibilidad que Pedro rechazará.)*

Take a look at the situation below:

Es importante (necesario) que los condutores respeten las señales de tránsito. (It is important (necessary) that drivers respect traffic signals.)

Teresita quería que Pedring le prestara dinero. (Teresita wanted Pedring to lend him money.)

The subjunctive mood is also used to express empathy. For expressing condolences or feeling sorry for another person's mishap but unable to do anything about it, the subjunctive mood is used. *(El modo subjuntivo también es usado para expresar la empatía. Para expresar condolencias o compadecer a la desgracia de otra persona pero incapaz de hacer algo sobre ello, el modo subjuntivo es usado.)*

Siento que hayas perdido tu vuelo. (I am sorry [that] you (have) missed your flight.)

In expressing certainty on the part of the primary subject, the verbs pensar (to think) and creer (to believe) are used. In this regard, the subjunctive becomes unnecessary. Meanwhile, the lack of belief does not necessarily remove the possibility of an event occurrence that is why the subjunctive is still used. *(En la expresión de la certeza de parte del sujeto primario, los verbos pensar (para pensar) y creer (para creer) son usados. En este aspecto, el subjuntivo se hace innecesario. Mientras tanto, la carencia de creencia no necesariamente quita la posibilidad de un acontecimiento de acontecimiento por eso el subjuntivo todavía es usado.)*

Consider the following sentence:

María cree (piensa) que existen los fantasmas, pero yo no pienso (creo) que existan. (María believes (thinks) ghosts exist, but I don't think (believe) that they do.)

Whenever the subject is directly related in action per se, there is no more a need to incorporate a subjunctive clause. The verb in its infinitive form is utilized in the main clause. . *(Siempre que el sujeto esté directamente relacionado en la acción en sí, no hay más una necesidad de incorporar una cláusula subjuntiva. El verbo en su forma de infinitivo es utilizado por lo general cláusula.)*

Observe the following sentences:

> Quiero que (tú) aprendas español. (I want you to learn Spanish)

> Quiero aprender español. (I want to learn Spanish.)

D. IMPERATIVE MOOD
(MODO IMPERATIVO)

While the indicative mood is for things that happened, is happening and will happen, and the subjunctive mood is for wishes and desire, the imperative mood is for the things one ought to do. Commands and requests use the imperative mood. *(Mientras el humor indicativo es para cosas que pasaron, pasan y pasarán y el modo subjuntivo es para deseos y deseo, el humor imperativo son para las cosas que habría que hacer. Las órdenes y las peticiones usan el humor imperativo.)*

Commands can either be affirmative or negative. In Spanish, they can be formal or informal. Informal commands are usually directed at someone whom the speaker would address as "tú" like a child, a family member, a good friend. On the other hand, formal commands are directed towards someone who would be addressed as "usted" such as an elder, a teacher, an officer, the president, and a new acquaintance. *(Las órdenes pueden ser o afirmativas o negativas. En Español, ellos pueden ser formales o informales. Las órdenes informales son por lo general dirigidas a alguien a que el altavoz se dirigiría como "tú" como un niño, un miembro de familia, un amigo bueno. Por otra parte, las órdenes formales son dirigidas hacia alguien que sería dirigido como "usted" como un mayor, un profesor, un oficial, el presidente, y un nuevo conocido.)*

Here are some examples of informal commands:

AFFIRMATIVE

habla (talk)

come (eat)

siéntate (sit down)

NEGATIVE

no hables (don't talk)

no comas (don't eat)

no te sientes (don't sit down)

Here are some examples of formal commands or requests:

AFFIRMATIVE

hable (talk)

siéntese (sit down)

coma (eat)

NEGATIVE

no hable (don't talk)

no coma (don't eat)

no se siente (don't sit down

Remember that formal commands usually use subjunctive verb forms as if they are sending out that there is a possible refusal on the other party. In this case, formal affirmative commands are usually requests. Moreover, even in negative commands, subjunctive forms are also used. (*(Recuerde que las órdenes formales por lo general usan formas de verbo subjuntivas como si ellos envían esto hay una respuesta negativa posible en el otro partido. En este caso, las órdenes afirmativas formales son por lo general peticiones. Además, hasta en órdenes negativas, las formas subjuntivas también son usadas.)*

Commands and requests may also be addressed to a group. Subjunctive form is again used to show that the group has the chance to refuse if they do not want to (*Las órdenes y las peticiones también pueden ser dirigidas a un grupo. La forma subjuntiva otra vez es usada para mostrar que el grupo tiene la posibilidad para negarse si ellos no quieren):*

AFFIRMATIVE

hablemos (let's talk)

comamos (let's eat)

entémonos (let's sit down)

hablad (talk)

med (eat)

sentaos (sit down)

hablen (talk)

coman (eat)

siéntense (sit down)

NEGATIVE

no comáis (don't eat)

no os sentéis (don't sit down)

no hablen (don't talk)

no coman (don't eat)

no se sienten (don't sit down)

no comamos (let's not eat)

no hablemos (let's not talk)

no nos sentemos (let's not sit down)
no habléis (don't talk)

E. INDICATIVE VS. SUBJUNCTIVE
(INDICATIVO VS. SUBJUNTIVO)

When it comes to verbal moods, think of two separate timelines that are running parallel to each other. The indicative mood is one where things have actually happened in the past, are happening in the present and will happen in the future. Meanwhile, the other timeline is called subjunctive. It is where things may or may not happen or may or may not have happened – like desires. The subjunctive mood is a plethora of uncertainties, while the indicative one is always grounded in reality. In practice, a subjunctive clause always depends, at least implicitly, on an indicative statement; they are linked by a conjunctive element, most often "que."
Consider the following example:

Es posible que vaya a México en verano. (It is possible that I will go to Mexico in the summer.)

Generally speaking, the subjunctive is used to converse about situations that go beyond the control of a sentence's primary subject. It is outcome is mostly uncertain. It is more like a wish. One example of this is when we expect drivers to arrive at a full stop in stop signs, but it does not necessarily mean that they will. We wish for it to happen, but it depends still. It is the same way as Teresita wanting to lend the money to Pedring, but there is still a possibility that Pedro will refuse. Take a look at the situation below:

Es importante (necesario) que los condutores respeten las señales de tránsito. (It is important (necessary) that drivers respect traffic signals.)

Teresita quería que Pedring le prestara dinero. (Teresita wanted Pedring to lend him money.)

The subjunctive mood is also used to express empathy. For expressing condolences or feeling sorry for another person's mishap but unable to do anything about it, the subjunctive mood is used.

Siento que hayas perdido tu vuelo. (I am sorry [that] you (have) missed your flight.)

In expressing certainty on the part of the primary subject, the verbs pensar (to think) and creer (to believe) are used. In this regard, the subjunctive becomes unnecessary. Meanwhile, the lack of belief does not necessarily remove the possibility of an event occurrence that is why the subjunctive is still used.

Consider the following sentence:

> María cree (piensa) que existen los fantasmas, pero yo no pienso (creo) que existan. (María believes (thinks) ghosts exist, but I don't think (believe) that they do.)

Whenever the subject is directly related in action per se, there is no more a need to incorporate a subjunctive clause. The verb in its infinitive form is utilized in the main clause.

Observe the following sentences:

> Quiero que (tú) aprendas español. (I want you to learn Spanish)
>
> Quiero aprender español. (I want to learn Spanish.)

F. IMPERATIVE MOOD
(MODO IMPERATIVO)

While the indicative mood is for things that happened, is happening and will happen, and the subjunctive mood is for wishes and desire, the imperative mood is for the things one ought to do. Commands and requests use the imperative mood. Commands can either be affirmative or negative. In Spanish, they can be formal or informal. Informal commands are usually directed at someone whom the speaker would address as "tú" like a child, a family member, a good friend. On the other hand, formal commands are directed towards someone who would be addressed as "usted" such as an elder, a teacher, an officer, the president, and a new acquaintance.

Here are some examples of informal commands:

AFFIRMATIVE

habla (talk)

come (eat)

siéntate (sit down)

NEGATIVE

no hables (don't talk)

no comas (don't eat)

no te sientes (don't sit down)

Here are some examples of formal commands or requests:

AFFIRMATIVE
hable (talk)

siéntese (sit down)

coma (eat)

NEGATIVE
no hable (don't talk)

no coma (don't eat)

no se siente (don't sit down)

Remember that formal commands usually use subjunctive verb forms as if they are sending out that there is a possible refusal on the other party. In this case, formal affirmative commands are usually requests. Moreover, even in negative commands, subjunctive forms are also used.

Commands and requests may also be addressed to a group. Subjunctive form is again used to show that the group has the chance to refuse if they do not want to:

AFFIRMATIVE·

hablemos (let's talk)

comamos (let's eat)

entémonos (let's sit down)

hablad (talk)

med (eat)

sentaos (sit down)

hablen (talk)

coman (eat)

siéntense (sit down)

NEGATIVE

no comáis (don't eat)

no os sentéis (don't sit down)

no hablen (don't talk)

no coman (don't eat)

no se sienten (don't sit down)

no comamos (let's not eat)

no hablemos (let's not talk)

no nos sentemos (let's not sit down)

no habléis (don't talk)

G. FUTURE MOOD
(MODO FUTURO)

You will probably not write a futuristic novel but it is important to know how to express an action that is yet to happen in Spanish. *(Usted no escribirá probablemente una novela futurista pero es importante saber expresar una acción que debe pasar aún en español.)*

In the upcoming sections, you will be introduced to a couple of ways to describe the future or "near future" by utilizing what you already know. These are sort of mock future tenses. We then show you how to form the future tense with regular and irregular verbs. *(En las secciones próximas, usted será presentado en un par de modos de describir el futuro "o el futuro próximo" utilizando lo que usted ya sabe. Éstos son la clase de futuros fingidos. Entonces le mostramos como formar el futuro con verbos regulares e irregulares.)*

Whenever implying something about the future, the present tense is used especially when asking for directions or whenever the proposed action will happen in a time that is not very distant or when the action will happen in the near future. *(Implicando algo sobre el futuro, el presente es usado sobre todo pidiendo direcciones o siempre que la acción propuesta pase en un tiempo que no es muy distante o cuando la acción pasará en el futuro próximo.)*

Consider the following examples:

¿Dejo de hablar? (Shall I stop talking?)

Ellos pasan por nuestra casa. (They'll be stopping by our house.)

EXPRESSING THE NEAR FUTURE WITH IR + A

Whenever expressing something that will take place in the near future or soon, use the present tense of the verb ir (to go) + the preposition a (which, in this case, has no meaning) + the infinitive of the verb. Take a look at the following examples that express what the subject is going to do *(Siempre que exprese algo que ocurrirá en el futuro cercano o pronto, use el tiempo presente del verbo ir (ir) + la preposición a (que, en este caso, no tiene significado) + el infinitivo del verbo. un vistazo a los siguientes ejemplos que expresan lo que el sujeto va a hacer)*:

Voy a salir. (I'm going to go out.)

Vamos a esperarlos. (We are going to wait for them.)

The present tense of ir is irregular, and you conjugate it as follows:

ir (to go)

voy

vamos

vas

vais

va

van

FUTURIZING REGULAR VERBS

One of the easiest tenses to form in Spanish is the future tense. This is because all verbs, regular or irregular, have the same future endings. Depending on the subject, regular future tense verbs simply take the entire -ar, -er, or -ir verb in its infinitive form and add the appropriate ending. When you are able to memorize all the endings, you can now be able to slay your Spanish class! (*Uno de los tiempos más fáciles para formarse en español es el futuro. Este es porque todos los verbos, regulares o irregulares, tienen los mismos futuros finales. Según el sujeto, los verbos de futuro regulares simplemente toman-ar entero,-er, o el verbo-ir en su infinitivo forma y añade el final apropiado. ¡Cuándo usted es capaz de memorizar todos los finales, usted puede ser capaz ahora de matar su clase española!*)

Future endings for all verbs:

yo −é

nosotros -emos

tú −ás

vosotros -éis

él, ella, Ud. -á

ellos, ellas, Uds. −án

EXAMPLES! The words that follow show how you form the future of some regular verbs with the endings from the previous table (*¡EJEMPLOS! Las palabras que siguen el espectáculo como usted forma el futuro de algunos verbos regulares con los finales de la mesa anterior*):

:

trabajar (to work)

trabajaré

trabajaremos

trabajarás

trabajaréis

trabajará

trabajarán

vender (to sell)

yo venderé

nosotros venderemos

tú venderás

vosotros venderéis

él, ella, Ud. venderá

venderán

discutir (to discuss, argue)

yo discutiré

nosotros discutiremos

tú discutirás

vosotros discutiréis

él, ella, Ud. discutirá

discutirán

Here are some sentences that use the future tense *(Aquí están algunas oraciones que usan el future):*

Yo no los invitaré a mi fiesta. (I won't invite them to my party.)

Ellos no beberán alcohol. (They won't drink alcohol.)

FUTURIZING WITH IRREGULAR VERBS

While setting verbs in the future tense is the easiest, some Spanish verbs are irregular in the future tense. These verbs have irregular future stems and they always end in -r or –rr. That is the easiest way to remember them! *(Poniendo verbos en lo venidero tensan es lo más fácil, algunos verbos españoles son irregulares en lo venidero tensan. Estos verbos tienen futuros tallos irregulares y ellos siempre terminan en-r o-rr. ¡Es el modo más fácil de recordarlos!)*

There are three ways to form the future of irregular verbs. You can do one of the three things *(Hay tres modos de formar el futuro de verbos irregulares. Usted puede hacer una de las tres cosas):*

1. **Before adding the future ending discussed in futurizing regular verbs, you can add an r to the stem of the verb.**

Infinitive	Meaning	Future Stem
caber	to fit	cabr-
poder	to be able	podr-
querer	to want	querr-
saber	to know	sabr-

Check out the following sample sentences:

¿Cabrá esa máquina en el gabinete? (Will that machine fit in the cabinet?)

No podremos venir. (We won't be able to come.)

Querré verlo. (I'll want to see it.)

¿Sabrá hacerlo? (Will he know how to do it?)

2. **You can add the letters -dr to the verb stem before adding the proper future ending:**

Infinitive	Meaning	Future Stem
poner	to put	pondr-
salir	to leave	saldr-
tener	to have	tendr-
valer	to be worth	valdr-
venir	to come	vendr-

The following sentences use the irregular verbs following the condition above.

Yo pondré los papeles en la mesa. (I'll put the papers on the table.)

¿Cuándo saldrán? (When will they leave?)

Ella no tendrá bastante dinero. (She won't have enough money.)

¿Cuánto valdrá ese coche? (How much will that car be worth?)

¿No vendrás mañana? (Won't you be coming tomorrow?)

3. **The third thing that you can is do is if verbs are in the third group of future irregulars and have irregular stems, you must simply memorize and then add the proper future endings:**

Infinitive	Meaning	Future Stem
decir	to say	dir-
hacer	to make, to do	har-

The verbs are used in the following sentences.

Yo diré lo que pienso. (I'll say what I think.)

¿Qué harán para resolver el problema? (What will they do to solve the problem?)

FORETELLING, PREDICTING, AND WONDERING WITH THE FUTURE TENSE
(ANULAR, PREDECIR Y MARAVILLAR CON EL TIEMPO FUTURO)

Expressing the future statements with the use of the future tense can be obvious. However, there are also other ways that you can use the future tense in Spanish. Just observe the following statements (*La expresión de las futuras declaraciones con el uso del futuro puede ser obvia. Sin embargo, hay también otros caminos que usted puede usar el futuro en español. Sólo observe las declaraciones siguientes*):

To say what somebody is about to do:

>Yo te ayudaré. (I'll help you.)

To predict a future action or event:

>Lloverá pronto. (It will rain soon.)

It can also be used to express wonder, probability, conjecture, or uncertainty in the present.

The Spanish future, in this case, is equivalent to the following English phrases: "I wonder," "probably," or "must be." Here are a few examples:

>¿Cuánto dinero tendrán? (I wonder how much money they have.)

>Serán las seis. (It's probably [It must be] six o'clock.)

>Alguien viene. ¿Quién será? (Someone is coming. I wonder who it is.)

>¿Será mi esposo? (I wonder whether it's my husband.)

>¿Irá a darme un anillo mi novio? (I wonder whether my boyfriend is going to give me a ring.)

To express something that you expect and that is due to or caused by a present action or event:

The Spanish future, in this case, is equivalent to the following English phrases: "I wonder," "probably," or "must be." Here are a few examples:

¿Cuánto dinero tendrán? (I wonder how much money they have.)

Serán las seis. (It's probably [It must be] six o'clock.)

Alguien viene. ¿Quién será? (Someone is coming. I wonder who it is.)

¿Será mi esposo? (I wonder whether it's my husband.)

¿Irá a darme un anillo mi novio? (I wonder whether my boyfriend is going to give me a ring.)

To express something that you expect and that's due to or caused by a present action or event:

Si viene a tiempo el jefe no se quejará. (If you come on time, the boss won't complain.)

Si sigues la receta prepararás una buena comida. (If you follow the recipe, you'll prepare a good meal.)

H. VERB RULES
(REGLAS VERBALES)

For pronunciation purposes, some Spanish verbs undergo spelling changes to preserve the original sound of the verb after having been added a new ending. This change is often nothing to be overly concerned about since it occurs only in the first-person singular (yo) form of the verb. *(Para objetivos de pronunciación, algunos verbos españoles se someten a cambios que saben escribir correctamente para conservar el sonido original del verbo habiendo sido añadido un nuevo final. Este cambio no es a menudo nada para estar demasiado preocupado por ya que esto ocurre sólo en la primera persona singular (yo) la forma del verbo.)*

In the present tense, verbs shown below undergo spelling changes. Refer to the list below *(En el presente, los verbos mostrados abajo se someten a cambios que saben escribir correctamente. Refiérase a la lista abajo):*

75

Infinitive Ending	Spelling Change	Verb Examples	Present Conjugation
vowel + -cer/-cir	c ⇒ zc	ofrecer (to offer)	yo ofrezco
		traducir (to translate)	yo traduzco
consonant + -cer/-cir	c ⇒ z	convencer (to convince)	yo convenzo
		esparcir (to spread out)	yo esparzo
-ger/-gir	g ⇒ j	escoger (to choose)	yo escojo
		exigir (to demand)	yo exijo
-guir	gu ⇒ g	distinguir (to distinguish)	yo distingo

Most of the verbs that undergo spelling changes in the present tense end in vowel + -cer or vowel + -cir. Only a few high-frequency verbs fall under the other categories (-ger, -gir, -guir); in all likelihood, you'll see them rarely, if at all. *(La mayor parte de los verbos que se someten a cambios que saben escribir correctamente al final de presente en vocal-cer o vocal-cir. Sólo unos verbos de alta frecuencia se caen bajo las otras categorías (-ger,-gir,-guir); en toda la probabilidad, usted los verá raramente, si en absoluto.*

Here are the verbs with spelling changes in the present tense that you can expect to encounter most often *(Aquí están los verbos con la ortografía de cambios del presente que usted puede esperar encontrar el más a menudo):*

Spanish Verb	Translation
aparecer	to appear
conocer	to know (to be acquainted with)
merecer	to deserve, merit
nacer	to be born
obedecer	to obey
parecer	to seem
producir	to produce

reconocer   to recognize

reducir   to reduce

reproducir   to reproduce

STEM-CHANGING VERBS

A number of Spanish verbs undergo stem changes, this means that there are changes in the stem of the verb. Note that the stem of the verb is what remains when the −ar, -er, or −ir ending has been taken off. In the present tense, all stem changes are applicable in all of the conjugated forms except for the nosotros and vosotros forms. *(Varios verbos españoles se someten a cambios de tallo, este significa que hay cambios del tallo del verbo. Note que el tallo del verbo es lo que permanece cuando el-ar,-er, o final de-ir ha sido quitado. En el presente, todos los cambios de tallo son aplicables en todas las formas conjugadas excepto formas de vosotros y el nosotros.)*

-ar stem changes

As stated above, the only exception are nosotros and vosotros and many Spanish verbs with an −ar do undergo stem changes. The list below details these changes:

e ⇒ ie: For instance, empezar (to begin) changes to yo empiezo (nosotros empezamos).

Here are the sample Spanish verbs that are frequently used and also fit into this category:

- cerrar (to close)
- comenzar (to begin)
- despertar (to wake up)
- negar (to deny)
- nevar (to snow)
- pensar (to think)
- recomendar (to recommend)

o/u ⇒ ue: For instance, mostrar (to show) changes to yo muestro (nosotros mostramos), and jugar (to play) changes to yo juego (nosotros jugamos). Here are the most frequently used Spanish verbs that fit into this category:

- acordar (to agree)
- acostar (to put to bed)

- almorzar (to eat lunch)
- colgar (to hang up)
- contar (to tell)
- costar (to cost)
- encontrar (to meet)
- probar (to try [on])
- recordar (to remember)

Jugar is the only common -ar verb whose stem vowel changes from u to ue. Consider the following sentences:
- Yo juego al fútbol. (I play soccer.)
- Julio y yo jugamos al golf. (Julio and I play golf.)

-er stem changes
Spaning verbs ending with –er undergo stem changes in all forms except nosotros and vosotros. The following list shows these changes *(Los verbos españoles que se terminan con-er se someten a cambios de tallo de todas las formas excepto nosotros y vosotros. La lista siguiente muestra estos cambios)*:

e ⇒ ie: Consider this, querer (to wish, want) changes to yo quiero (nosotros queremos). Here are the most frequently used Spanish verbs that fit into this category:
- defender (to defend)
- encender (to light)
- entender (to understand)
- perder (to lose)

o ⇒ ue: For instance, volver (to return) changes to yo vuelvo (nosotros volvemos). Here are the most frequently used Spanish verbs that fit into this category:
- devolver (to return)
- doler (to hurt)
- envolver (to wrap up)
- llover (to rain)
- poder (to be able to, can)

Some verbs with stem changes in the present tense are used impersonally in the third-person singular only:

> Llueve. (It's raining.) (llover; o ⇒ ue)
>
> Nieva. (It's snowing.) (nevar; e ⇒ ie)
>
> Hiela. (It's freezing.) (helar; e ⇒ ie)
>
> Truena. (It's thundering.) (tronar; o ⇒ ue)

-ir stem changes

Many Spanish verbs with an -ir ending undergo stem changes in all forms except nosotros and vosotros. The following list outlines these changes *(Muchos verbos españoles con un final de-ir se someten a cambios de tallo de todas las formas excepto nosotros y vosotros. La lista siguiente perfila estos cambios):*

e ⇒ ie: For instance, preferir (to prefer) changes to yo prefiero (nosotros preferimos). Here are the most frequently used Spanish verbs that fit into this category:

- advertir (to warn)
- consentir (to allow)
- divertir (to amuse)
- mentir (to lie)
- sentir (to feel, regret)
- sugerir (to suggest)

o ⇒ ue: For instance, dormir (to sleep) changes to yo duermo (nosotros dormimos). Another verb conjugated like dormir is morir (to die).

e ⇒ i: For instance, servir (to serve) changes to yo sirvo (nosotros servimos). Here are the most frequently used Spanish verbs that fit into this category:

- despedir (to say goodbye to)
- expedir (to send)
- medir (to measure)
- pedir (to ask for)
- repetir (to repeat)
- vestir (to clothe)

Stem change for verbs ending in -iar

Some Spanish verbs with an -iar ending undergo a stem change in all forms except nosotros and vosotros. This stem change is i ⇒ í. For instance, guiar (to guide) changes to yo guío (nosotros guiamos). Here are the most frequently used Spanish verbs that fit into this category *(Algunos verbos españoles con un final de-iar se someten a un cambio de tallo de todas las formas excepto nosotros y vosotros. Este cambio de tallo es yo ⇒ í. Por ejemplo, guiar (para dirigir) se cambia a yo guío (nosotros guiamos). Aquí están los verbos españoles el más con frecuencia usados que caben en esta categoría)*:

> enviar (to send)
> esquiar (to ski)
> fotografiar (to photograph)
> vaciar (to empty)

LET'S EXERCISE!

Fill in the table with the correct form of the verb group corresponding to the pronouns modified. The first one is already filled out. *(Rellene la mesa con la forma correcta del grupo de verbo correspondiente a los pronombres modificados. El primer es llenado ya.)*

	-ar	-er	-ir
I	hablo	como	vivo
he/she/it/you (Vd.)			
we			
they/you (Vds.)			

A LITTLE TEST

Now that you have been introduced to the different moods namely: subjunctive, indicative, and imperative. It is now time for you to try answering some exercises. *(Ahora que usted ha sido presentado en los humores diferentes a saber: subjuntivo, indicativo e imperativo. Esto es ahora el tiempo para usted para tratar de contestar algunos ejercicios.)*

For the following sentences, conjugate the verb in parentheses in the present tense of the indicative mood. *(Para las oraciones siguientes, conjugue el verbo en paréntesis en el presente del humor indicativo.)*

1. ¡Hola! ¿Cómo _____ (estar) hoy? (Hello! How are you today?)
2. Mi nombre _____ (ser) Juan y _____ (ser) de España. (My name is Juan, and I am from Spain.)
3. Mis amigos y yo _____ (querer) visitar la ciudad. (My friends and I want to visit the city.)
4. Tú y tu novia _____ (poder) venir con nosotros, si _____ (querer). (You and your girlfriend can come with us if you want to.)
5. Le _____ (tener) que preguntar a ella, pero _____ (creer) que dirá que sí. (I have to ask her, but I think that she will say yes.)
6. ¿A dónde _____ (pensar, ustedes) ir primero? (Where are you thinking of going first?)
7. ¿Por qué no _____ (ir, nosotros) al museo de arte moderno? (Why don't we go to the modern art museum?)
8. Escuché que _____ (haber) una exhibición de Pablo Picasso muy interesante. (I heard there is a very interesting Pablo Picasso exhibit.)
9. ¿Qué tal si luego _____ (comer, nosotros) en el centro? (What if afterwards, we eat downtown?)
10. ¡Excelente idea! (conocer) un buen restaurante de mariscos. (Excellent idea! I know a good seafood restaurant.)

For the following sentences, conjugate the verbs in parentheses in the preterit tense of the indicative mood. *(Para las oraciones siguientes, conjugue los verbos en paréntesis en el tiempo de preterit del humor indicativo.)*

1. El verano pasado _____ (estar, yo) en Mexico por seis semanas. (Last summer I was in Mexico for six weeks.)
2. _____ (ser) uno de los viajes más divertidos de mi vida. (It was one of the most fun trips of my life.)
3. _____(conocer, yo) a mucha gente e _____ (hacer) muchos amigos. (I met many people and made many friends.)
4. ¿_____ (comer, tú) mucha comida mexicana? (Did you eat a lot of Mexican food?)

5. _____ (probar) de todo, ¡hasta chapulines fritos en Oaxaca! (I tried everything, even fried grasshoppers in Oaxaca!)

6. ¿Qué cosas _____ (ver, tú)? ¿Qué lugares _____ (visitar, tú)? (What things did you see? What places did you visit?)

7. La familia con la que _____ (quedarse, yo) me _____ (llevar) a todas partes. (The family that I stayed with took me everywhere.)

8. _____ (subir, nosotros) a las pirámides de Tulúm y _____ (bucear) en Cancún. (We climbed the pyramids in Tulúm and scuba dived in Cancún.)

9. Suena como que _____ (divertirse, tú) mucho. (It sounds like you had a lot of fun.)

10. Sí, me _____ (dar) tristeza pero al final _____ (tener, yo) que regresar a casa. (Yes, it made me sad to leave but in the end I had to come back home.)

For the following sentences, conjugate the verbs in parentheses in the future tense of the indicative mood. *(Para las oraciones siguientes, conjugue los verbos en paréntesis en lo venidero el tiempo del humor indicativo.)*

1. ¿Adónde _____ (ir, vosotros) de vacaciones este verano? (Where will you all go on vacation this summer?)

2. No lo _____ (saber, nosotros) hasta el ultimo minuto. (We won't know until the last minute.)

3. Pero en cuanto sepáis me lo _____ (decir, vosotros), ¿no? (But as soon as you all know you will tell me, won't you?)

4. ¿Para qué? De cualquier manera no _____ (poder, tú) venir con nosotros. (What for? You won't be able to come with us anyway.)

5. No, pero finalmente _____ (tener, yo) un poco de paz y tranquilidad. (No, but I will finally have some peace and quiet.)

For the following sentences, conjugate the verbs in parentheses in the present perfect tense of the indicative mood. . *(Para las oraciones siguientes, conjugue los verbos en paréntesis en el tiempo de pretérito perfecto del humor indicativo.)*

1. ¿Alguna vez _____ (estar, tú) enamorado de alguien? (Have you ever been in love with someone?)
2. No, nunca _____ (querer, yo) a nadie en mi vida. (No, I have never loved anyone in my life.)
3. Nunca le _____ (decir, yo) palabras de amor a nadie. (I have never said words of love to anyone.)
4. Nadie me _____ (escribir) ni yo _____ (abrir) una carta de amor nunca. (No one has written me nor have I opened a love letter ever.)
5. Parece que tu vida _____ (ser) muy triste hasta ahora. (It seems that your life has been very sad until now.)
6. Pero _____ (tener, yo) muchos buenos amigos y _____ (hacer, yo) muchas cosas. (But I have had many good friends, and I have done many things.)
7. Simplemente no _____ (poner, yo) mucho esfuerzo en el aspecto romántico de mi vida. (I simply haven't put much effort in the romantic aspect of my life.)
8. Por lo menos tampoco _____ (romperse) muchos cora-zones por mi culpa. (At least not many hearts have been broken because of me.)
9. Y ¿_____ (resolver, tú) hacer algo al respecto de tu vida amorosa? (And have you resolved to do something about your love life?)
10. Todo lo que puedo decir es que no _____ (morir, yo) todavía. (All that I can say is that I haven't died yet.)

For the following sentences, conjugate the verbs in parentheses in the present tense of the subjunctive mood.

1. ¿Qué quieres ser cuando _____ (ser, tú) grande? (What do you want to be when you grow up?)
2. Sólo espero que en el futuro todavía _____ (haber) recursos naturales suficientes. (I only hope that in the future there are still sufficient natural resources.)
3. Es probable que el planeta _____ (tener) muchos más problemas de los que tiene ahora. (It's probable that the planet may have many more problems than it has now.)
4. ¡Necesitamos que los líderes del mundo _____ (hacer) algo ahora! (We need the world leaders to do something now!)

5. ¿Crees que a ellos les importa lo que tú _____ (pensar) o
_____ (decir, tú)? (Do you think that they care what you may think
or say?)

For the following sentences, conjugate the verbs in parentheses in the past tense of the subjunctive mood. *(Para las oraciones siguientes, conjugue los verbos en paréntesis en el pasado del modo subjuntivo.)*

1. No puedo creer que nadie _____ (estar) consciente del peligro. (I can't believe that no one was aware of the danger.)
2. Yo pedí muchas veces que alguien _____ (hacer) una investigación completa. (I requested many times that someone do a thorough investigation.)
3. Supongo que nadie pensaba que algo así _____ (poder) pasar. (I suppose that nobody thought that something like this could happen.)
4. o quizá alguien les ordenó a los empleados que no _____ (decir) nada. (Or maybe someone ordered the employees not to say anything.)
5. Si yo _____ (ser) tú, trataría de involucrar a los medios en el asunto. (If I were you, I would try to get the media involved in the matter.)

For the following sentences, use the appropriate imperative form of the verb in parentheses. *(Para las oraciones siguientes, use la forma imperativa apropiada del verbo en paréntesis.)*

1. ¡Anda! _____ (llevar + me, inf.) al cine esta noche. (Come on! Take me to the movies tonight.)
2. Bueno, pero no _____ (tardarse, inf.) mucho en salir de la casa. (All right, but don't take too long getting out of the house.)
3. ¡No _____ (ser, inf.) pesado! (Don't be a pain!)
4. _____ (dar+nos, for.) dos boletos para la función de las ocho, por favor. (Give us two tickets for the eight o'clock show, please.)
5. No le _____ (poner, for.) mucha mantequilla a las palo-mitas, por favor. (Don't put too much butter on the popcorn, please.)

DOUBLED VOCABULARY AND PHRASES FOR PRACTICING SPANISH

(VOCABULARIO DOBLADO Y FRASES PARA PRACTICAR EL ESPAÑOL)

PHRASES FOR PRACTICING SPANISH

Here are some phrases that you can practice on for speaking Spanish. These are basic phrases and sentences with the correct pronunciation to better guide you in verbal Spanish. *(Aquí están algunas frases con las cuales usted puede practicar para decir el español. Éstos son frases básicas y oraciones con la pronunciación correcta para dirigirle mejor en el español verbal.)*

padre (pah-dreh) (father)
madre (mah-dreh) (mother)
hijo (ee-Hoh) (son)
hija (ee-Hah) (daughter)
hermano (ehr-mah-noh) (brother)
hermana (ehr-mah-nah) (sister)
yerno (yehr-noh) (son-in-law)
nuera (nooeh-rah) (daughter-in-law)
nieto (neeeh-toh) (grandson)
nieta (neeeh-tah) (granddaughter)
cuñado (koo-nyah-doh) (brother-in-law)
cuñada (koo-nyah-dah) (sister-in-law)
primo (pree-moh) (cousin [male])
prima (pree-mah) (cousin [female])
padrino (pah-dree-noh) (godfather)
madrina (mah-dree-nah) (godmother)
tío (tee-oh) (uncle)
tía (tee-ah) (aunt)

abuelo (ah-bvooeh-loh) (grandfather)

abuela (ah-bvooeh-lah) (grandmother)

oy mujer. (sohy moo-Hehr) (I'm a woman.)

Soy Canadiense. (sohy kah-nah-dee-ehn-seh) (I'm Canadian.)

Soy de Winnipeg. (sohy de Winnipeg) (I'm from Winnipeg.)

Ellos son muy altos. (eh-yohs sohn mooy ahl-tohs) (They're very tall.)

¿Ustedes son Uruguayos? (oos-teh-dehs sohn oo-roo-gooah-yohs) (Are you [formal] Uruguayan?)

Ella es maestra. (eh-yah ehs mah-ehs-trah) (She's a teacher.)

Eres muy bella. (eh-rehs mooy bveh-yah) (You're very beautiful.)

Eres muy gentil. (eh-rehs mooy Hehn-teel) (You're very kind.)

¿Quién? (keeehn) (Who?)

¿Qué? (keh) (What?)

¿Dónde? (dohn-deh) (Where?)

¿Cuándo? (kooahn-doh) (When?)

¿Por qué? (pohr keh) (Why?)

¿Cómo? (koh-moh) (How?)

¿Cuánto? (kooahn-toh) (How much?)

¿Cuál? (kooahl) (Which?)

¿Quién es él? (keeehn ehs ehl) (Who is he?)

¿Qué hace usted? (keh ah-seh oos-tehd) (What do you do?)

¿Dónde viven? (dohn-deh bvee-bvehn) (Where do you [plural]/they live?)

¿Cuándo llegaron? (kooahn-doh yeh-gah-rohn) (When did you [plural]/they arrive?)

¿Por qué está aquí? (pohr keh ehs-tah ah-kee) (Why are you [formal] here? Why is he/she/it here?)

¿Cómo es el camino? (koh-moh ehs ehl kah-mee-noh) (What's the road like?)

¿Cuánto cuesta el cuarto? (kooahn-toh kooehs-tah ehl kooahr-toh) (How much is the room?)

¿Cuál hotel es mejor? (kooahl oh-tehl ehs meh-Hohr) (Which hotel is better?)

Muchas gracias. (moo-chahs grah-seeahs) (Thank you very much.)

No, gracias. (no grah-seeahs) (No, thank you.)

Nada, gracias. (nah-dah grah-seeahs) (Nothing, thanks.)

Lo siento. (loh seeehn-toh) (I'm sorry.)

Mi culpa. (mee kool-pah) (My fault.)

Con permiso. (kohn pehr-mee-soh) (Excuse me. [in the way])

Discúlpeme. (dees-kuhl-peh-meh) (Excuse me. [interrupt])

¿Qué necesita usted? (keh neh-seh-see-tah oos-tehd) (What do you need?)

Quiero unas baterías. (keeeh-roh oo-nahs bah-tehr-ee-ahs) (I want some batteries.)

¿Habla usted inglés? (ah-bvlah oos-tehd een-glehs) (Do you speak English?)

Hablo inglés. (ah-bvloh een-glehs) (I speak English.)

¿Habla usted español? (ah-bvlah oos-tehd eh-spah-nyohl) (Do you speak Spanish?)

Hablo español. (ah-bvlah eh-spah-nyohl) (I speak Spanish.)

No entiendo. (noh ehn-teeehn-doh) (I don't understand.)

No hablo mucho español. (no ah-bvloh moo-choh eh-spah-nyohl) (I don't speak much Spanish.)

¿Repita, por favor? (reh-pee-tah pohr fah-bvohr) (Can you repeat that, please?)

Necesito información, por favor. (neh-seh-see-toh een-fohr-mah-see-ohn pohr fah-bvohr) (I need information, please.)

Necesito ayuda. (neh-seh-see-toh ah-yoo-dah) (I need some help.)

¿Adónde va usted? (ah-dohn-deh bvah oos-tehd) (Where are you going?)

No sé. (noh seh) (I don't know.)

¡Buen provecho! (bvooehn proh-bveh-choh) (Enjoy your meal! — the equivalent of the French Bon appetit!)

¿Con qué está servido? (kohn keh ehs-tah sehr-bvee-doh) (What does it come with?)

Está caliente. (ehs-tah kah-leeehn-teh) (It's hot [temperature].)

Está frío. (ehs-tah freeoh) (It's cold.)

Está picante. (ehs-tah pee-kahn-teh) (It's hot [flavor/spice].)

Es sabroso. (ehs sah-bvroh-soh) (It's tasty.)

Lamento, no tenemos . . . (lah-mehn-toh noh teh-neh-mohs) (Sorry, we don't have . . .)

¿Qué ingredientes tiene? (keh een-greh-deeehn-tehs teeeh-neh) (What are the ingredients?)

¿Qué más trae el plato? (keh mahs trah-eh ehl plah-toh) (What else is in the dish?)

Escoger un vino. (ehs-koh-Hehr oon bvee-noh) (Choose a wine.)

¡Salud! (sah-lood) (Cheers!)

Tomar un refresco. (toh-mahr oon reh-frehs-koh) (Drink a soda pop.)

Tomar un trago. (toh-mahr oon trah-goh) (Have a drink [alcoholic].)

Un vaso de agua. (oon bvah-soh deh ah-gooah) (A glass of water.)

Un vaso de leche. (oon bvah-soh deh leh-cheh) (A glass of milk.)

Ahora no, gracias. (ah-oh-rah noh grah-seeahs) (Not now, thank you.)

Ya tengo, gracias. (yah tehn-goh grah-seeahs) (I already have some [or it], thanks.)

No me interesa, gracias. (no meh een-teh-reh-sah grah-seeahs) (It doesn't interest me, thank you.)

Más tarde, gracias. (mahs tahr-deh grah-seeahs) (Later, thank you.)

No me gusta, gracias. (noh meh goos-tah grah-seeahs) (I don't like it, thanks.)

No me moleste, ¡por favor! (noh meh moh-lehs-teh pohr fah-bvohr) (Don't bother me, please!)

el arroz (ehl ah-rrohs) (the rice)

el atún (ehl ah-toon) (the tuna)

el fideo (ehl fee-deh-oh) (the pasta)

los cereales (lohs seh-reh-ah-lehs) (the cereals)

las galletas (lahs gah-yeh-tahs) (the cookies or crackers)

la leche (lah leh-cheh) (the milk)

pagar (pah-gahr) (to pay)

el pasillo (ehl pah-see-yoh) (the aisle)

las sardinas (lahs sahr-dee-nahs) (the sardines)

el vino (ehl bvee-noh) (the wine)

el vuelto (ehl bvooehl-toh) (change [as in money back]); la vuelta (lah bvooehl-tah) in Spain

las ollas (lahs oh-yas) (pots)

el tercer pasillo (ehl tehr-sehr pah-see-yoh) (the third aisle)

al fondo (ahl fohn-doh) (at the back)

Gracias, aquí está su vuelto. (grah-seeahs ah-kee ehs-tah soo bvooehl-toh) (Thanks, here's your change.)

¿Dónde está la entrada? (dohn-deh ehs-tah lah ehn-trah-dah) (Where's the entrance?)

¿Dónde está la salida? (dohn-deh ehs-tah lah sah-lee-dah) (Where's the exit?)

empuje (ehm-poo-Heh) (push)

tire (tee-reh) (pull)

jale (Hah-leh) (pull [in Mexico])

el ascensor (ehl ah-sehn-sohr) (the elevator)

la escalera mecánica (lah ehs-kah-leh-rah meh-kah-nee-kah) (the escalator)

el vendedor (ehl bvehn-deh-dohr) or la vendedora (lah bvehn-deh-doh-rah) (the salesperson [male and female])

la caja (lah kah-Hah) (the check-out stand)

DOUBLED VOCABULARY

Here are some words with English-Spanish translation to better orient you with the Spanish verb vocabulary. *(Aquí están algunas palabras con la traducción inglés-española para orientarle mejor con el vocabulario de verbo español.)*

admit - confesar

abandon - dejar

abuse - abusar

accept- aceptar

accomplish - cumplir

accuse- acusar, culpar

achieve-alcanzar, conseguir, lograr

act- actuar

administer - administrar

admire- admirar

admit - admitir, reconocer

adore - adorar

agitate - revolver

agree - aceptar, concordar

aid- ayudar, socorrer

allocate - repartir

allow - permitir

allow entry - admitir

amaze - admirar

analyze - analizar

announce-declarar, participar

answer-contestar, responder

apply - aplicar

apply for - solicitar

appoint - nombrar

appreciate - apreciar

approve - aprobar

argue - discutir

arm - armar

arouse - despertar

arrange - arreglar, disponer, ordenar, organizar

arrest - detener

arrive - aterrizar, llegar

ask - encargar, preguntar

ask for - pedir

aspire - pretender

assemble - armar

assist - asistir, auxiliar

assume - suponer

appoint - nombrar

appreciate - apreciar

approve - aprobar

argue - discutir

arm - armar

arouse - despertar

arrange - arreglar, disponer, ordenar, organizar

arrest - detener

arrive - aterrizar, llegar

ask - encargar, preguntar

ask for - pedir

aspire - pretender

assemble - armar

assist - asistir, auxiliar

assume - suponer

attain - lograr

attempt - intentar

attend - asistir

attract - captar

avoid - evitar

avoid something - huir

awaken-despertar, encender

back away - retroceder

back down - retroceder

bake - cocer, hornear

ban - prohibir

battle - batallar

be - estar, ser

be (age, measure) - tener

be able to - poder

be admitted - ingresar

be afraid - temer

be alike - parecerse

be born - nacer

be concerned - preocuparse

be confident - confiar

be detrimental - perjudicar

be fond of - apreciar

be glad - alegrarse

be happy - alegrarse

be inattentive - descuidar

be lacking - carecer

be mad about - enloquecer

be moved - emocionarse

be of use for - servir

be opposed - oponerse

be promising - prometer

be quiet- callarse

be relieved - aliviarse

be sorry- lamentar, sentir

be sufficient - alcanzar

be unaware of - ignorar

be unsuccessful - fracasar

be wrong - equivocarse

bear - aguantar, cargar, resistir, soportar, sufrir

beat - batir, golpear

become sad - entristecerse

beg - pedir, rogar, suplicar

begin - comenzar, empezar, iniciar, principiar

behave - comportarse

believe - creer

beseech- suplicar

betray - vender

bite - morder

blame - culpar

block - tapar

board - embarcarse

boast - presumir

boil - cocer, hervir

boo - chiflar

bother - molestar

bounce - saltar

bow - rendirse

brake - frenar

break - romper

break up - cortar, deshacer

breathe - respirar

bribe - comprar

brighten up - endulzar

bring - traer

bring down - derribar

brush - cepillar

buckle - abrochar

build - construir

button up - abrochar

buy - comprar

call - llamar

calm down - calmarse

can - poder

caress - acariciar

carry - cargar, llevar, transportar

carry on - proseguir

carry out - cumplir

cash - cobrar

catch - alcanzar, atrapar, coger, prender

cause - traer

celebrate - celebrar

change - cambiar

change (clothes) - mudarse

charge - acusar, cargar, cobrar

chase - perseguir

chat - conversar

cheat - copiar

cheat on - engañar

check - checar, repasar, revisar

chew - masticar

choose - elegir, escoger

chop - cortar

churn - batir

claim - reclamar

clarify - aclarar

clean - lavar, limpiar

clear - borrar, limpiar

clear up - aclarar

climb - escalar, subir, trepar

close - cerrar

clothe - vestir

collaborate - colaborar

collect - cobrar, coleccionar, juntar, recoger

collide - chocar

combine - conjugar

come - acudir, llegar, venir

come/go back - volver

come down - bajar

come up with - inventar

command - mandar

commit - cometer

commit suicide - suicidarse

compare - comparar

complain-protestar, reclamar

compose - componer

comprehend - comprender

conceal - ocultar

concur- concordar

confess - confesar

confirm - confirmar

conjugate - conjugar

connect - conectar

consider - considerar, estudiar, juzgar

construct - construir

consume - consumir

continue - continuar, proseguir, seguir

contribute - contribuir

control - controlar, regir

convince - convencer

cook - cocer, cocinar

cooperate - colaborar

copy - copiar, imitar

correct- corregir, reparar

count - contar

cover - comprender, tapar

crash - chocar

create - crear

creep up - trepar

criticize - criticar

cross - atravesar, cruzar, pasar

cry - llorar

cure - curar

cut- cortar

damage - dañar, perjudicar

dance - bailar

dare - osar

date - salir

deal with - tratar

debate - discutir

deceive - engañar

decide - decidir, resolver

declare - declarar

deduce - deducir

deduct- deducir

defeat - vencer

delete - borrar

deliver - entregar

demand - reclamar

demolish - derribar

demonstrate - demostrar

deny - negar

deposit - ingresar

descend- descender

describe - describir

deserve - merecer

desire - desear

despair - desesperarse

despise - despreciar

destroy - destruir

detain - detener

detest - detestar

develop-desarrollar, elaborar

die - morir

direct - dirigir

disappear - desaparecer

disarm - desarmar

discover - descubrir

discuss - discutir

dismantle - desarmar

dispatch - euviar

display - mostrar

distinguish - distinguir

distribute - repartir

disturb - molestar

dive - bucear

do - hacer

do again - volver

do research - investigar

do up - abrochar

doubt - dudar

download - bajar

draw - dibujar

dread - temer

dream - soñar

dress - vestir

dress up - disfrazarse

drink - beber, tomar

drive - conducir, empujar, manejar, mover

drive insane - enloquecer

drop - tirar

dub - doblar

dwell - habitar, morar

earn - cobrar, ganar

ease off - calmarse

eat- comer

elect - elegir

eliminate - eliminar

embark on - emprender

embrace - abrazar

employ - emplear

end - acabar, terminar

end up - terminar

endure - aguantar, padecer

engrave - grabar

enjoy - disfrutar, gozar

enjoy oneself - divertirse

enter - entrar, ingresar

erase - borrar

escape - escapar, huir

etch - grabar

examine - examinar, explorar

excuse - disculpar, perdonar

expect - esperar, pretender

expel - echar

expire - vencer

explain - explicar

explore - explorar

express - expresar

express an opinion - opinar

fail - fallar, fracasar

faint-desfallecer, desmayarse

fall - caer, descender

fall ill - enfermarse

fall in love - enamorarse

fasten - abrochar

fatten - engordar

fear - temer

feel - sentir

feel faint - desfallecer

feign - fingir

fight - batallar, luchar, pelear

fill - llenar

find - encontrar, hallar

find out - averiguar, descubrir, investigar

finish - acabar, terminar

fit - caber

fix - arreglar, composer, reparar

flee - huir

flirt - coquetear

flush - jalar

fly - volar

fold - doblar

follow - seguir

forbid - prohibir

force - obligar

forget - olvidar

forgive - disculpar, perdonar

fuel - cargar

fulfill - cumplir

gain - captar, ganar

get - captar, coger, conseguir, obtener, procurar, recibir, sacar

get angry - enojarse

get away - escapar

get better - aliviarse

get bored - aburrirse

get closer - acercar

get dirty- ensuciar

get drunk - emborracharse

get even - desquitarse, empatar

get exasperated - desesperarse

get excited - emocionarse

get from - heredar

get ill - enfermarse

get infected - contagiarse

get mad - enojarse

get married - casarse

get out- quitar, salir

get rid of - eliminar

get sick - enfermarse

get thin - enflacar

get tired - cansarse

get up early - madrugar

get upset - emocionarse

give - dar, entregar

give (a speech) - pronunciar

give a talking to - regañar

give away - regalar

give back - devolver, regresar

give up - rendirse

go - acudir, ir

go across - cruzar

go ahead - andar

go back - regresar

go by - pasar

go crazy - enloquecer

go down - bajar, descender

go on - continuar

go on board - embarcarse

go or come in - entrar

go out - salir

go over - repasar

go past - pasar

go through - atravesar

go to bed - acostarse

go up - subir

go wrong - fallar

govern - goberuar

grade - corregir

grasp - captar

greet - saludar

grow - crecer

grow sad - entristecerse

guard - vigilar

guess - adivinar

halt - detener

hand out - repartir

handle - manejar, tocar

hang - colgar

happen - pasar

harm - dañar, perjudicar

hate - detestar, odiar

have - poseer, tener

have an early dinner- merendar

have a feeling - intuir

have a good time - disfrutar, divertirse

have an afternoon snack - merendar

have available - disponer

have breakfast - desayunar

have dinner - cenar

have fun - divertirse, gozar

have to - deber

heal - curar

hear - escuchar, oír, sentir

help - auxiliar, ayudar, socorrer

hesitate - dudar

hide - esconder, ocultar

hinder- impedir

hire - alquilar

hit - golpear, pegar

hobble - cojear

hold - sostener, teuer

hold (capacity) - caber

honor - distinguir

hope - esperar

hug - abrazar

hunt - cazar

hurt - herlr, lastimar

ignore - ignorar

imagine - imagitiar

imitate - copiar, imitar

impede - impedir

implore - suplicar

include - comprender

increase - elevar

indicate - indicar

inherit - heredar

initiate - iniciar

insist - insistir

inspect - examinar, revisar

interfere - interferir

introduce - presentar

invent - inventar

invest - invertir

investigate - investigar

invite - invitar

involve - suponer

join - ingresar, juntar

journey - viajar

judge - juzgar

jump - brincar, saltar

keep - conservar, guardar

keep an eye on - vigilar

keep on - seguir

key in (type) - teclear

kick - patear

kill - matar

kill oneself - suicidarse

kiss - besar

knit - tejer

knock - llamar

knock down - derribar

know - conocer, entender, saber

know how - saber

labor - laborar

lack - carecer, faltar

land - aterrizar

laugh - reir

launch - lanzar

lay - colocar

leap - saltar

learn - aprender, estudiar

lease - alquilar, rentar

leave - dejar, salir

leave out - omitir

lend - prestar

let - dejar

let go - soltar

let know - avisar

lie - mentir

lie (dead) - yacer

lie down - acostarse

lift- elevar, levantar

light - encender, prender

limp - cojear

link - conectar

listen - escuchar, oír

live - vivir

live in - habitar
load - cargar
locate - situar
look - mirar, ver
look after - cuidar
look down on - despreciar
look for - buscar
look like - parecerse
loose heart - desfallecer
lose - extraviar, perder
lose weight - enflacar
love - adorar, amar, querer
lower - bajar
maintain - sostener
make - cometer, elaborar, fabricar, hacer, preparar
make a living - vivir
make a mistake - equivocarse
make possible - permitir
make the most of - aprovechar
make up - inventar
manage - administrar, dirigir, lograr, regir
manipulate - manejar
manufacture - fabricar
match - empatar
may - poder
measure - tener
meddle - interferir
meet - conocer, reunirse
memorize - memorizar
mention - nombrar
mislead - engañar
misplace - extraviar
miss - fallar, faltar

mix - batir, mezclar, revolver

moor - amarrar

move - mover

move (dwelling) - mudarse

move back - retroceder

murmur - susurrar

must - deber

name - nombrar

narrate - narrar

need - faltar, necesitar

neglect - descuidar

note - notar

notice - notar, reparar

notify - avisar

obey - obedecer, respetar

object - oponerse

observe - observar

obtain - conseguir, obteuer

offer - ofrecer

omit - omitir

open - abrir, destapar

ordain - ordenar

order - disponer, encargar, mandar, ordenar, pedir

organize - organizar

overcome - vencer

owe - deber

own - poseer

paint - pintar

participate - participar

pass - pasar

pass (an exam) - aprobar

pay - pagar

pay attention - atender

penalize - castigar

perceive - percibir

perform - celebrar, practicar, representar

permit - permitir

persevere - perseverar

persist- perseverar

persuade - convener

phone - llamar

pick - coger, escoger

pick up - recoger

pin - prender

place - colocar

plan - planear

plane (wood) - cepillar

play - jugar, practicar

play (a musical instrument) - tocar

plug in - enchufar

possess - poseer

post - situar

practice - ensayar, practicar

pray - rezar, rogar

predict - presumir

prefer - preferir

prepare - elaborar, preparar

present - presentar

present (as a gift) - regalar

preserve - conservar

pretend - finger, pretender

prevent - evitar, impedir

print - imprimir

produce - elaborar, fabricar

prohibit - prohibir

promise - prometer

pronounce - pronunciar

propose - proponer, sugerir

protect- proteger, resguardar

protest- protestar

prove- demostrar, probar

provide - proveer

pull- jalar

punish- castigar

purchase - comprar

pursue- perseguir

push - empujar

put - colocar, echar, poner

put away - guardar

put back - reponer

put in - meter

put into practice - aplicar

put on makeup - maquillarse

put on or gain weight- engordar

put the lid (cap. cover) on - tapar

put together - armar, juntar

put up - colgar

put up with - sufrir

quarrel - pelear

quit - renunciar

raise - elevar, levantar, subir

reach - alcanzar, llegar

read - leer

recall - recordar

receive - percibir, recibir

recognize - reconocer

recommend - sugerir

reconnoiter - reconocer

record - grabar

recover - recobrar, rescatar

recycle - reciclar

reflect - reflexionar

refuse - negar, rehusar

regain - recobrar

regret - lamentar, sentir

rehearse - ensayar

reject - despreciar, rechazar

relate - narrar

relax - relajarse

release - soltar

remain - quedarse

remember - acordarse, recordar

remind - recordar

remove - eliminar, quitar

renounce - renunciar

rent- alquilar, rentar

repair - arreglar, componer, reparar

repel - rechazar

replace - remplazar, reponer

reply - contestar, responder

represent - representar

request - rogar, solicitar

require - necesitar, obligar

rescue - rescatar

resemble - parecerse

reserve - reservar

reside - morar, residir

resign - renunciar

resist- resistir

resolve - resolver, solucionar

respect - respetar

respond- obedecer, responder

rest - descausar

retrieve - recobrar

return - devolver, regresar, volver

reunite - reunirse

reveal - descubrir

reverse - invertir

review - criticar, repasar, revisar

revolve - girar

ride - montar

rip- desgarrar

rise - crecer

ruin- destruir

rule- gobernar, regir

rule (legal) - fallar

run - correr, dirigir

run away - escapar, huir

run into (something)- chocar, tropezar

safeguard - resguardar

salute - saludar

save - ahorrar, evitar, guardar, rescatar

say - decir, rezar

say good-bye - despedirse

say hello - saludar

scale - escalar

scold - regañar

scout - explorar

scratch - rascar

scream - gritar

search- buscar

see - apreciar, ver

select - escoger

sell - vender

sell out - vender

send - enviar, mandar

sense- intuir, percibir

serve- atender, servir

set- poner, situar

set out - empreuder

set sail- zarpar

set up - poner

set up with - euchufar

settle - resolver

shake - temblar

share - compartir

shave - afeitarse

shed - derramar

shiver - temblar

should - deber

shout - gritar

shove - empujar

show - demostrar, ensenar, indicar, mostrar

shudder- temblar

shut - cerrar

shut up - callarse

sigh - suspirar

signify - representar

simulate - imitar

sing - contar

sit - sentarse

sketch- dibujar

skip- brincar

slacken - relajarse

sleep - dormir

slow down - frenar

smash - romper

smell- oler

smoke - fumar

sneeze- estornudar

snore- roncar

soften - endulzar

soil - ensuciar

solve - resolver, solucionar

sort out - arreglar, enderezar

spare - ahorrar

speak - hablar

spend - gastar

spew out - vomitar

spill- derramar

spin- girar

stand- resistir, soportar

start- comenzar, empezar, entrar, iniciar, principiar

state - declarar, expresar

stay - quedarse

stay awakev- desvelarse

stick - pegar

stipulate - disponer

stir - revolver

stop - detener, frenar, parar

stop doing something - dejar

straighten - enderezar

stroke - acariciar

struggle- batallar, luchar

study- estudiar, examinar

stumble - tropezar

substitute - remplazar

succeed to - heredar

suffer- padecer, sufrir

suggest - proponer, sugerir

sully - ensuciar

summon - llamar

sunbathe - asolearse

supply- proveer

support - apoyar, soportar, sostener

suppose- presumir, suponer

surf (Web) - explorar

surrender - rendirse

survive - sobrevivir

suspect - sospechar

swap - cambiar

swear- jurar

sweat- sudar

sweep - barrer

sweeten- endulzar

swell - engordar

swim - nadar

switch off - apagar

switch on - encender, enchufar

symbolize - representar

take - coger, llevar, tomar

take (a long) time - tardar

take (a picture) - sacar

take a bath - banarse

take a lid off - destapar

take a walk (a stroll) - pasear

take advantage of - abusar

take apart - desarmar

take away - quitar

take care - cuidar, encargar

take into account - considerar

take out-sacar

take part - participar

take pleasure - gozar

talk - conversar, hablar

taste - probar

teach- enseñar

tear - desgarrar, romper

tell - contar, decir

tell - narrar

tend to- atender

test - ensayar, probar

testify - declarar

think - creer, opinar, pensar, reflexion ar

throw- aventar, echar, lanzar, tirar

throw away - tirar

throw up - devolver, vomitar

tidy up- ordenar, recoger

tie - amarrar, atar, empatar

tolerate - aguantar

toss - tirar, voltear

touch - tocar

train - entrenarse

translate - traducir

transport - transportar

travel - viajar

treat - iuvitar, tratar

tremble - temblar

trip - tropezar

trust - confiar

try - ensayar, intentar, probar, procurar

try to - tratar

turn - doblar, girar, voltear

turn (age) - cumplir

turn down - rechazar

turn in - entregar

turn off - apagar, cerrar

turn on - poner, preuder

turn over - voltear

turn to - acudir

type - teclear

unblock- destapar

uncover- descubrir

understand - comprender, engender

undertake - embarcarse, empren der

undo - desatar, deshacer

unleash - desatar

untie - desatar, deshacer

uphold - sostener

upset - molestar

use - aprovechar, emplear, usar, utilizar

utilize - utilizar

vanish - desaparecer

visit - visitar

vomit - vomitar

vote - votar

wait - esperar

wake - despertar

walk - andar, caminar

want - desear, querer

warn - avisar

wash - lavar

waste- desperdiciar, gastar

watch - mirar, observar, vigilar

wear - llevar, traer, usar, vestir

weave - tejer

weigh anchor - zarpar

welcome - recibir

whisper - susurrar

whistle - chiflar

win - ganar

wish - desear

wobble - cojear

work - andar, laborar, trabajar

worry- preocuparse

worship - adorar

wound - herir

wreck - destruir

write - escribir

welcome ...... recibir

whisper - susurrar

whistle - chiflar

win -.. ganar

wish -. desear

wobble - cojear

work -. andar, laborar, trabajar

worry-. preocuparse

worship - adorar

wound - herir

wreck - destruir

CONCLUSION

(CONCLUSIÓN)

Learning a second language is not that easy but you have to admit that it is challenging. Aside from your native language, it is quite challenging to learn about a very unfamiliar language like the Spanish Language. *(Aprender un segundo idioma no es tan fácil, pero debes admitir que es un desafío. Además de su idioma nativo, es bastante difícil aprender sobre un idioma muy desconocido como el español.)*

Here, you have learned the correct pronunciation of some Spanish words, the proper gestures that must accompany the statement that you are making, and also the use of verbs, pronouns, nouns, adjectives, adverbs, prepositions and the like. Through this tool, you have learned all grammatical factors without enrolling in a formal class-type review of Spanish Language. *(Aquí, ha aprendido la pronunciación correcta de algunas palabras en español, los gestos adecuados que deben acompañar a la declaración que está haciendo, y también el uso de verbos, pronombres, sustantivos, adjetivos, adverbios, preposiciones y similares. A través de esta herramienta, ha aprendido todos los factores gramaticales sin inscribirse en una revisión formal de clase de español.)*

Furthermore, there are also short stories which make the learning even more exciting. Through some tips in reading, you will surely find Spanish Language reading and learning enjoyable instead of considering it as a burden. *(Además, también hay historias cortas que hacen que el aprendizaje sea aún más emocionante. A través de algunos consejos en lectura, seguramente encontrará agradable la lectura y el aprendizaje del idioma español en lugar de considerarlo como una carga.)*

The use of short stories may be considered as designed for kids or children who are learning through baby steps, but the truth is that a learner of second language is considered as baby steps too. There is no harm in considering it as a kid-like way of learning. That is again a form of humility. Remember that humility is the start of learning. *(El uso de cuentos cortos puede considerarse diseñado para niños o niños que están aprendiendo a través de pequeños pasos, pero la verdad es que un aprendiz de segundo idioma también se considera como pequeños pasos. No hay daño en considerarlo como una forma de aprendizaje infantil. Esa es nuevamente una forma de humildad. Recuerda que la humildad es el comienzo del aprendizaje.)*

As parting words, you should always carve in your mind that learning is one way of showing humility because you are admitting into yourself that you still have a lot to learn and that will make you even more fit to perfect your goal – in this instance, the Spanish Language and Grammar. *(Como palabras de despedida, siempre debes recordar que aprender es una forma de mostrar humildad porque admites en ti mismo que todavía tienes mucho que aprender y que te hará aún más apto para perfeccionar tu objetivo; en este caso, Lengua y gramática española.)*

CPSIA information can be obtained
at www.ICGtesting.com
Printed in the USA
BVHW050759120521
607047BV00003B/464